HOW TO FIND THOSE HIDDEN JOBS

by

Violet M. Cooper

DIMI PRESS   **Salem, Oregon**

DIMI PRESS
3820 Oak Hollow Lane, SE
Salem, Oregon 97302

Printed in the United States of America

This edition first printed March, 1995
10 9 8 7 6 5 4 3 2 1

Price: $13.95

Library of Congress Cataloging in Publication Data;
      Cooper, Violet M.,
           How to find those hidden jobs / by Violet M. Cooper
              p.   cm.
           Includes index.
           ISBN 0-931625-25-4 (pbk.) : $13.95
           1. Job hunting. I. Title.
      HF 5382.7.C667   1995
      650.1'4--dc20   650.14   94-40677
                                       CIP

Cover design by Bruce DeRoos
Original cartoons by SueAnn Walker
'Memory Joggers' design by Terry Wright
Typeface 12 pt. Times

OTHER DIMI PRESS PRODUCTS FOR YOU

ORDER FORM

Name _____

Address _____

City/State/Zip _____

Phone _____

Enclosed is my check for $16.95 ($13.95 for *HOW TO FIND THOSE HIDDEN JOBS* and $3 for shipping).

DIMI PRESS
3820 Oak Hollow Lane, SE
Salem, OR 97302-4774

Phone 1-800-644-DIMI(3464) for orders
or 1-503-364-7698 for further information
or FAX to 1-503-364-7698
or by INTERNET to dickbook@aol.com

Call toll-free and order now!

To my dear sister and special friend,

Doras Briggs

I built castles in the air.

Doras put foundations under them.

FOREWORD

Today's job market is different than the one our parents faced. It takes more than training or a college degree to become successfully employed in a rewarding career.

The key to survival in today's job market is to have access to good information; not only occupational and industrial trends but also career goal-setting and job-search techniques.

Violet Cooper has written an extemely valuable book for those who are in the midst of making career choices. She has an easy-to-read style sprinkled with examples from her real-life experiences as a job and career counselor.

Ms. Cooper shows us step-by-step how to take advantage of those visible and hidden job opportunities that are just waiting for somebody to come along.

I recommend this book for the first-time job seeker, the worker permanently laid off, the employed-but-looking-for-something-better, as well as the retired-but-restless.

There is a world of satisfying and rewarding opportunities for the reader who is faithful in pursuing the innovative, logical, and proven job-search and career-decision techniques outlined in this book

Earl Fairbanks
Labor Economist

CONTENTS

Jobs always develop from a need...the
employer's need, not yours. Jobs may be
invisible for a number of reasons, the principal reason being that the employer lists his
jobs in what he has found is the most effective way to generate good prospects.

The Dictionary of Occupational Titles lists
standard and alternate titles for the cluster
of tasks you can do.

The job title may be non-descriptive. Find
out what the employer really wants.

Common jobs often appear in uncommon
places.

Plan No. 2: Build New Jobs for Yourself

Strategy # 5. Reassemble Your Skills

> Rearrange your skills and give the new structures new titles. This process creates new job opportunities for you.

Plan No. 3: Find a Need and Fill It

Strategy # 6: Be a Problem Solver

> Your problem solving abilities are assets to offer an employer. Employers hire problem solvers.

Plan No. 4: Organize a Network

Strategy # 7. Set Up a Personal Network

> Several pairs of eyes and ears will generate more job possibilities than you can alone.

Strategy # 8. Advertise for Ideas

> A bold approach. Offer a reward for information on a variety of related jobs.

Strategy # 9. Contribute to a Job Bank

> "Deposits" consist of information about current job openings. "Withdrawals" come

when members make use of the
information to apply for jobs.

Plan No. 5: Check the Employers' "Want List"

Strategy # 10. Learn Who's Recruiting Your
Skills

Strategy # 11. Use CPC's Job Choices Annual
for Clues

Clues to competitive industries or
businesses in your area.

Strategy # 12. Consult Annual for Out-of-Area
Jobs

Strategy # 13. Use Annual to Identify Employers Who Want Your Degree and/
or Experience

Strategy # 14. Locate Opportunities for
Students

Strategy # 15. Research Your Potential
Employers

Find several niches where you will fit.

Plan No. 6: Get a Foot in the Door

Strategy # 16. Sign Up for Temporary Work

Strategy # 17. Try Part Time Work

Strategy # 18. Work for a Staff Leasing Company

Businesses are beginning to "rent" their employees.

Strategy # 19. Use Seasonal Jobs as an Entry

Strategy # 20. Apply for Co-op Education Program

Strategy # 21. Volunteer Your Skills or for Training

Strategy # 22. Win Friends to Influence People

The personal touch pays off.

Plan No. 7: Apply Where the Employer Looks

Strategy #23. Use the Channel the Employer Prefers

There is no standard method for locating applicants. Certain preferences can be roughly classified by industry.

x

PLAN NO. 1

EXPAND YOUR HORIZONS

Hunting a job rates right along with visiting the dentist and paying income taxes. It's undignified, anxiety-provoking, and frequently nonproductive. Besides, "there are no jobs!" Yet your brother-in-law got one. Your neighbor down the street starts next Monday, and your best friend made a successful change. They got jobs. You didn't.

What made the difference? Probably, all things being equal, each of them one way or another tapped into the hidden job market. You can do the same.

By now you may have exhausted the standard ways of job hunting. You have made regular visits to the State Employment Service. You've pored over the Help Wanted ads in the newspaper. You filled out applications until your patience and your pen gave out.

If you came away empty handed, you have only two options left:

1. Give up, or,
2. Try new strategies.

Until you've tried No. 2, No. 1 is unthinkable.

You can stand in line at the employment office, wait for the phone call that never comes, listen to politicians who are long on promises and short on delivery, and sit out a recession that never recedes... hoping for a fairy godmother.

Or... you can refuse to let somebody else pull the strings. You can take charge of your own life.

This means YOU manage what happens to you. YOU take the first step...and the second...and the third. YOU make the decisions. You control your destiny. If you fail, you take the blame. But if you succeed, the rewards are all yours.

Moving from being somebody's puppet to being your own person requires a radical change in your way of thinking. In fact, it may be a complete reversal. Instead of waiting for something to happen, YOU are going to make things happen. Instead of limiting yourself, YOU are going to expand your capabilities. Instead of believing what "THEY" say, (whoever "THEY" are), you are going to challenge these self-appointed authorities.

You are going to believe in yourself, trust your own good sense, and act on it. I'll show you the way. I can't walk it for you. You can come with me or not. The decision is yours. Let's begin...

To take charge means to initiate action. It means YOU make the first move, not the employer. It means YOU plan the strategy, not wait for somebody else to map out your steps. It means YOU locate the information you need and make your own decisions. No longer will someone else do your thinking for you. It means to try, to fail, then to pick yourself up and try again.

In the present labor market, getting a job demands breaking out of the old ruts and thinking differently. It's a buyer's market, and the employer is doing the buying. When business is bad, the employer stops buying and starts cutting back. What worked fifteen, ten, or even five years ago is not working today.

There are plenty of things needing fixing in our world. The process of fixing we call "work". There is work out there. Lots of it. As long as the employer has an unfilled need, you have a chance of getting a job. If we didn't need a paycheck, employers would be competing for our help. It's the work-plus-salary that creates the problem.

Logically, if you can make money or save money for the employer, he will be looking for you. By "employer," I mean a business, an industry, a government entity, a school, and even a customer when you're self-employed.

AS LONG AS THE EMPLOYER HAS AN
UNFILLED NEED, YOU HAVE A CHANCE
OF GETTING A JOB.

Jobs always develop from a need... the employer's need or the customer's need, not yours. That's why advertisements announcing job openings are titled "Help Wanted".

Your talents are your stock in trade. To put your talents to use, first...

GET RID OF THE NOTION THAT ALL JOBS ARE LISTED IN THE CLASSIFIED ADS OR WITH THE EMPLOYMENT SERVICE.

(When did you last see an ad in either place for a college president or a highwire artist?)

Statisticians for the Department of Labor will admit that the Employment Service probably lists between 10% and 20% of the available jobs on any given day. You, being a smart job hunter, can figure out that at least 80% of the jobs have to be located somewhere else.

Where are they? Jobs may be invisible for a number of reasons, the principal reason being that the employer lists his job in a different way. He shops for applicants in what he has found is the most effective way to generate good prospects.

So, obviously,

Remember, the employer looks for applicants in what he has found is the most efficient and cost effective way for him.

To do this, he may list only through...
PRIVATE EMPLOYMENT AGENCIES

Or, the applicant skills he wants are found at...
THE STATE EMPLOYMENT SERVICE

If his is a union shop, he is under contract to hire by way of ...
THE UNION HALL

If the work requires advanced academic training, he tries...
PROFESSIONAL SOCIETIES,
CONFERENCES, SEMINARS,
or RECRUITS at UNIVERSITIES.

In other situations, the employer encourages jobseekers to make direct application to his business, factory, or organization. That is, he prefers...
GATE HIRES

Civil service agencies—city, county, state, and federal—all have distinct hiring procedures of their own. You find out about their job openings usually through ...
PERSONNEL OFFICES

None of this is top secret. If you want to know how your occupation is filled by a specific company, pick up the phone. Talk to the personnel department, or whoever hires for that kind of work. Ask. Professional job developers do it all the time.

When you get this information from one employer, however, don't assume the process is the same for every similar employer. Remember, each one develops his own way of getting applicants. These ways can be different. This leads us to an obvious truth...

PEOPLE KNOW ABOUT JOBS, JOB CHANGES, JOBS VACATED, JOBS COMING UP, JOBS UNDER CONSIDERATION.

If you are serious about working for a specific company:

 * Talk with receptionists, secretaries, maintenance people, sales people. Any employees of the firm, past or present, can be helpful. Find out how they learned about their jobs.

 * Check bulletin boards. This includes the supermarket and the laundromat. Look at organizational bulletin boards, at churches, colleges, offices. (Some trucking

companies list jobs for truckers on the back of their highway haulers.)

* Read trade magazines, utility publications, college newspapers. Watch for conference and convention notices as well as specific job listings.

* Ask at the Chamber of Commerce for conventions in the area. Find out about planning boards, commissions, government agencies.

* Call Federal Job Information Centers listed in the telephone book.

* Call city, county, and state personnel offices or check job postings in their buildings.

* Read newspapers for purchases of new industry sites, contracts let, new products, personnel changes, expansions. Look through the free "throwaway" papers found usually near other newsracks outside supermarkets.

* Don't overlook business weeklies, regional sections of the Wall Street Journal, and display ads for job openings scattered throughout Sunday editions.

* Use your library for business information, for other newspapers in surrounding communities, for telephone books where you will find potential employers in the yellow pages.

* Consider plants, factories in industrial parks,

shopping centers, construction sites, and new office buildings. These are places to ask about jobs.

Be specific about the kind of work you want. Employers do not hire generalists. They hire for specific skills: janitorial help, sales help, nursing, supervising, shipping, research, etc. Telling an employer you "can do anything," is ludicrous, not to mention irrational. You can't "do anything." Nobody can.

The employer assigns a job title to a cluster of tasks, things he wants done on the job. Then he gives this cluster a name: Cook, Welder, Carpenter, Dancer, Accountant. You must think of yourself in terms of a job title or, better still, a series of job titles. This gives you a target to shoot at in your job search.

Strategy No. 2

An employer may call your work by a different name, so:
LEARN ALTERNATE TITLES FOR YOUR JOB

Job titles are supposed to help. Often they just muddy the waters. The employer can call a cluster of tasks anything he wants. That's why the garbage collector has become the "sanitary engineer". The general office clerk becomes the "private secretary," and a bus supervisor may be referred to as the "transportation administrator."

8

These euphemisms may give the worker a greater sense of self-importance, but such prestigious job titles also confuse the jobseeker. You need to know alternate titles.

The Department of Labor issues a Dictionary of Occupational Titles which describes some 20,000 occupations, their standard titles, and alternate titles. Few employers are aware of this resource, and fewer use it. Instead, each names his job whatever he wishes. Consequently, when you look for work under the title assigned you in a previous occupation, you may have trouble making a match between the old job and the new. So you need more information.

Go to your public library or the Employment Service office. Look at the D.O.T. (Dictionary of Occupational Titles). You may need some help with this. Ask for it. Your best bet is at the state employment service. Locate the kind of work you do. Then make a list of other names frequently used to identify this work.

Now you won't pass up job openings because you don't recognize your work under a different name. Let me illustrate:

Maybe you have been a Stock Clerk. Do you also apply for jobs such as Stock Checker, Stockroom Clerk, Storekeeper, Storeroom Clerk, Supply Room Clerk?

Or, are you a Machine Builder? Then you are also a Special Machine Assembler, a Bench Hand, a Fitter, a

Bench Machinist, and a Vise Hand. You may also be called a Tool Machine Set-up Operator, or a Fixture Builder.

A Manufacturer's Service Representative is often called a Field Engineer, a Field Servicer, a Service Engineer, or simply a Service Representative.

In a similar manner, a Survey Worker may also be an Interviewer, a Merchandising Representative, a Public Interviewer, or any other title an employer chooses.

If the employer can make up a title for the tasks he wants you to perform, you, too, can make up a title of your own for that same work.

Caution: BE REALISTIC. You must be able to back up your claims. (If you have taken simple bookkeeping courses, you cannot claim to be an accountant.)

Give your work several names, names that seem logical to you. Then look for job listings that have similar titles. These may be your job under aliases.

Read job descriptions. Lots of them. When one fits your skills, notice what this employer calls the work. Keep a list of alternate names for your work.

Strategy No. 3

READ JOB DESCRIPTIONS...
THOROUGHLY

Ignore job titles. This may seem a contradiction of "learn alternate job titles." What it really means is: Don't be unduly impressed by names tacked on job listings. Find out what the job is all about. Determine whether you can do it (and want to), then decide if you will apply.

I once saw a state civil service job posted at the Employment Service office with this title: "Assistant Public Guardian Conservator." Most applicants walked right on by. Those who stopped to read further saw this first line: "This is a new position with the coroner's office."

That did it. No one read the rest. This was unfortunate in a university community where there were a number of new graduates with degrees in social service. The complete description indicated that the job was a kind of surrogate parent position. Orphaned children or incapacitated elderly with no relatives require someone to oversee their needs. This was the role of the "Assistant Public Guardian Conservator," a social service job.

In another community, a city posted notices to hire "Rehabilitation Counselors." Of course, this meant working with the handicapped to assist them in getting employment. Wrong! The city was considering upgrading an area of abandoned ramshackle buildings. The "Rehabilitation Counselors" were inspectors who would assess the feasibility of renovating specific structures in the neighborhood.

To read job descriptions thoroughly, do this:

Look beyond the salary and closing date. Read the tasks.

   * Ask yourself: "Is this something I have done? Is it similar to what I have done? Have I done it in a different way? Have I done it under different circumstances?

   * Read descriptions for verbs. Does the employer want you to train, supervise, demonstrate, examine, install, operate, weld, compile, record, tend, trim, label, inspect, deliver... etc., etc.? Describe yourself in the job words on your application and résumé. Use the terms the employer uses as much as possible during the interview. He understands this language.

   * Does the employer hint that he would modify his expectations? Does he say your education may be "equivalent"? Does he suggest your experience, though not the same, may be "related"? Does he suggest your background can be "approximately" what he is asking?

You will find that job requirements are seldom set in concrete.

The moral of this story is: The title isn't everything.

Read the job content. You may be surprised.

Strategy No. 4

LOOK FOR YOUR JOB
IN AN UNUSUAL PLACE

Now that you have learned to look for your job in the job description, buried under a non-descriptive title, there are other places it may be concealed.

Shakespeare wrote: "All the world's a stage, and all the men and women merely players."

If we think of the whole world as our stage and jobs as the specific roles we play on the stage, then there must be more than one place, more than one industry, more than one business, where we can play out our work roles. And there is.

Let me give you an easy example:

An experienced hospital nurse arrived the first day at one of my career classes. She was going to change occupations. Her husband was tired of the irregular hours she worked. He wanted a more predictable life for the two of them.

"Do you like nursing?" I asked her.

"Oh, yes, I love it," she replied. "But I really need to spend more time with my husband."

"Well, have you thought of school nurse, college nurse, office nurse, industrial nurse, Red Cross nurse?" I asked.

She hadn't. Now she did. I lost a prospective student that day. She left happy, without attending a single session. She had her answer: Same occupation... new environment. As long as she lacked such information, these jobs, for her, were hidden.

Now, put your own work into a different setting... perhaps in the area of some special interest you have.

Martin did. He was an accountant. The ballet was his special interest. Since there was no foreseeable possibility of his ever being a dancer, he decided, nevertheless, to work surrounded by his interest. He applied for and got a job as business manager for a major ballet company.

Think about it. What's going on in the world about you? For example, new economic trends generate new needs, and therefore new jobs. Financial institutions are finding themselves with millions of dollars in foreclosures. This throws them into the property management field, and they are hiring skilled real estate managers to handle these new duties.

We find architects and engineers working for insurance companies... as architects and engineers. Why?

Because the insurance companies invest heavily in real estate.

We find helicopter pilots working for logging companies and Christmas tree farms, lifting logs and trees out of the less accessible areas to staging points. Helicopter pilots also work for mapping companies, radio stations, television crews, law enforcement agencies, and hospitals.

You know the most obvious occupations that are found in colleges and universities and hospitals and hotels. Do you know they also hire secretaries, mail clerks, painters, carpenters, and janitors? And don't forget purchasing agents, graphic artists, and public information specialists, to name some others.

Large religious organizations need more than the clergy. Bruce was not a man of the cloth. Bruce was a very successful stockbroker, but had a strong desire to contribute more to the welfare of his fellow man. His free time was spent with youth groups, with his church, and charitable organizations.

Soon it became apparent that he found his greatest enjoyment in these activities. He finally decided to forego his large income for the chance to stay with his special interests. Using his successful organizational skills, he is now business manager for a major theological seminary.

Phil, on the other hand, was a minister, but the demands of his ministerial calling left little time for his family. So the time came when he moved his counseling skills to the State Employment Service. Here he worked his forty hours a week and was free to spend weekends and holidays with his family.

And then there was Sue. Sue had some minor experience as an editor, and liked the work. But when she moved to the West Coast to a smaller community, the only position she could find was a secretarial job with the County Health Department. Not long into that position, she discovered that her immediate supervisor and others on the staff disliked writing the many reports expected of them.

At first Sue offered to help with the grammatical and spelling errors. Then she moved to writing portions of the reports. Finally she found herself accepted as writer and editor for the Health Department... another occupation in an unlikely place.

Probably the most improbable was Dorene's. Dorene hoped to apply her considerable musical and dramatic skills to earning a living. While I, as her employment counselor, searched the usual channels, Dorene called me to report she had found a job.

"Congratulations!" I was hearty in my approval. "What are you doing?"

"Encyclopedia sales," she replied happily.

"Encyclopedia sales!" I exploded in surprise.

"For school children," she amended. "I take my guitar when I go to call on a family. Then I tell the stories of children in foreign lands and sing their native songs." She laughed. "When I point out the pictures and interesting information about these children in other lands to my customers' children, I've made my sale."

Using her dramatic talents, Dorene brought a new dimension to her job. She sold a quality product, delighted her customers, and produced more orders for the employer. Within three months Dorene topped previous sales records.

Stereotyping limits job search. Instead, think imaginatively. Watch businesses and industries for the occupations behind the scenes. Your job may be hiding there.

* What goes on in a museum besides displaying artifacts?

* What goes on in an airline besides ticket sales and flying?

* What goes on in a newspaper besides reporting and editing?

* What goes on in a school district beyond teaching?

* What goes on behind the lobby of a convention hotel?

Nurses in industry? Accountants in ballets? Real estate managers in financial institutions? Architects and engineers working for insurance companies? A minister in job counseling? An editor in the health department? Drama and music in encyclopedia sales?

17

Do you also know that maintenance electricians and plumbers work on traveling Amtrak trains? Strange, but true.

Common jobs often appear in uncommon places. Yours may be one of them.

SUMMARY

We now have four ways to uncover "hidden" jobs:

1. Find out from the employer how he locates applicants for the job you want.

2. Find out from the Dictionary of Occupational Titles alternate titles for your work. Watch for these titles.

3. Find out exactly what the employer wants by ignoring job titles. Read content carefully.

4. Look for your job in an unusual place.

Knowing these four ways should open opportunities for you.

There are still more…

PLAN NO. 2

BUILD NEW JOBS FOR YOURSELF

A hidden job for most people is a non-existent job. Yet there are jobs going unfilled and job seekers going unemployed because the applicants, unknowingly, actually "hide" jobs from themselves.

If you keep hearing, " Sorry, we don't have an opening for your type of work," then it's time to create new kinds of work for yourself. How? By rearranging your skills and giving the new structure other titles. All legitimate. All valid.

You did the same thing as a child. You took a pile of building blocks, and, depending on your game, sometimes you built a bridge. Sometimes you erected a tower. Sometimes you tore the tower down, discarded some blocks, added others, and built a castle or a corral or a cabin. The same process creates new job opportunities for you.

To begin with, you need lots of building materials. Placement officers and employment specialists call these "marketable skills." You probably have been asked several times to "make an inventory of your skills." It's a good idea, but how do you go about it? And what, really, is a skill?

A skill can be an ability developed by formal training. A skill can be an activity for which you have been paid. A skill can be a specific technical competence. Or skills evolve from the tasks of a craft. But that's not all.

Your skills include all the means and methods by which you have accomplished day-to-day living. This means the way you deal with people, how you use information, and what you do with things. You started accumulating skills in childhood. You continue adding to your skills as an adult.

So, a thorough inventory of all these useful abilities gives you a wealth of materials from which to construct and perform other jobs. Let's see how this works.

Carol is employed as a general office clerk (her employer calls her "the bookkeeper") for a small automotive repair shop. The boss is retiring and the business will soon close. Carol is looking for another job.

In her present position, Carol makes out invoices, receipts, estimates, policies, statements, and payroll checks. She receives and pays out the inventory records and does the re-ordering. She computes wages and taxes and fills out checks to pay bills. She gives information to customers and adjusts complaints.

Carol also operates the office machines, the computer terminal, adding machine, a copy machine, and a fax machine. She opens the mail and prepares all the correspondence for her employer's signature. She purchases office supplies, answers the telephone, and runs errands.

All these skills Carol has listed on her personal inventory, but there is much more Carol has not considered.

After some prodding, Carol added these: She has been active as a 4-H leader and a Girl Scout leader. She often does volunteer work in community services. She writes promotion for her club and church, and plans programs and meetings.

In school she was deeply involved in the school newspaper, both as reporter and later as editor. She has considerable ability with crafts such as needlepoint, sewing, stained glass, and pottery. She has taught these skills to the children in her Scout and 4-H groups and at the summer camps where she was a camp counselor.

Carol has wide reading interests, and is particularly fascinated by behavioral science. She enjoys people, and studies behavior in individuals and groups. In her contacts with others Carol has exhibited a special skill in helping them solve their problems. Although she modestly disclaims this, Carol is also tactful and persuasive.

Persuasiveness cannot be measured by a time and accuracy test in the same way typing speed is determined, nevertheless persuasiveness is an important skill. Although communication skills may not be as visible as a set of balanced books, yet these talents are equally marketable. We often overlook the intangible abilities we have, and only count those skills that can produce something we can feel, see, touch, taste, or smell.

Carol now has identified a broader range of talents which will allow her to seek a variety of jobs confidently. It is obvious that she has four major skills areas: office skills, public contact skills (tact, diplomacy, persuasiveness, and teaching), arts and crafts skills (creativity, and hand and finger dexterity), and organizational skills. She is free to move into occupations which emphasize any of these. By picking one area, e.g., public contact, she does not forfeit the use of the rest of her talents. These will come into play as supportive or auxiliary abilities.

If Carol elects to do the same work she has been doing, she can apply for jobs under several titles. Some employers call her present tasks a "Girl Friday" job. Some call it "bookkeeper," "secretary," or "receptionist." More correctly, the Dictionary of Occupational Titles names this cluster of tasks: "administrative clerk" or "general office clerk."

However, if Carol wants to broaden the scope of her job search she can do so by emphasizing other skills in different combinations. For example, by combining her office skills with her experience with parents and children, plus her proven planning and organizing talents and her ability for responsible independent action, Carol might consider applying at the district office for a job as school secretary. At the university level this would be departmental secretary or division secretary.

Carol might draw on her strong interest in books and reading, and apply to be a library technical assistant. Here she would bring into play her inventory skills, her accuracy in record keeping, certainly her public contact skills.

She would provide information service, answer questions about the computerized catalogs, and assist the public. All these abilities are essential for the position of library technician.

Carol's talents in various hobby crafts and her persuasive teaching abilities and public contact experience come into focus in the position of recreation leader with the City Parks and Recreation District. Or Carol might decide to teach these skills to others at the Community College Adult School level. In this event she would apply for work as an instructor. Both of these positions require program planning, which is one of Carol's strengths. In addition, Carol would be a valuable asset to a craft shop owner or in a fabric shop.

There are other possibilities. Carol could use her writing and communication skills on a small daily or weekly newspaper. She might move to the other side of the Employment Service desk and become the employment interviewer where her skills in communication, persuasion, and problem solving would help others to find work.

By re-structuring task clusters (and, therefore, skill clusters) new jobs are formed. Carol, and you, need not have worked under a particular job title previously in order to apply for that job now. Whatever you have the ability to do (paid for or not), you have the right to try.

Tim, too, rearranged his skills into a new occupation. Tim was employed in hospital maintenance. He liked the work because it allowed him to use a wide variety of building crafts. It also appealed to his sense of independence, and he could schedule his own days.

Those were busy days. He constructed, erected, installed, and repaired doors, partitions, cabinets, shelves, counters, and the many other structures and fixtures needed in an active medical unit. He often drew the plans, prepared the layout, and ordered the materials as well as performing the specific construction. In addition, Tim supervised helpers and work/study students from a nearby community college.

At home, he designed and built furniture for his family. He particularly enjoyed this because here he was free to spend the time turning out precise and accurate work. Tim liked to create quality products.

When he was not at his bench, Tim enjoyed the outdoors. He spent as much time as he could spare at the seashore or the mountains. The solitude was to his liking, and he understood the fascination the outdoors held for the sportsman. All of this led to his decision to combine his two major interests: carpentry (furniture design), and outdoor recreation.

Of course he had highly developed carpentry skills, and he had successfully designed and completed a number of fine pieces of furniture. He tallied up the additional skills he could count on. He had an adequate knowledge of electricity and plumbing. He had done some flooring and panelling work for the hospital. He could read and understand blueprints and schematics. And, he knew from experience the special needs of families who wanted to travel and camp outdoors.

In Tim's mind, this added up to designing and constructing custom-made recreational vehicles. He applied for and got a job with a company which specialized in just such equipment.

Had Tim not found this position, there are a number of alternatives for which his skills qualify him: furniture assembler; recreation vehicle repairer; cabinetmaker; building maintenance man in offices, apartments, schools, industry, and even convention centers, fairgrounds, or federal and state parks.

His supervisory experience in which he taught helpers and students the techniques of his trade points to instructing classes in fine cabinetry for adults.

What Carol and Tim have done, you can do. Now collect your building blocks...a lot of them. Include not only your paid-for skills, but those intangibles you have overlooked. Think back, even to your childhood. What have you done, and probably still do (though in a more adult form), that brought you Brownie points, a gold star, a commendation, a sense of success, accomplishment, and satisfaction? Often you will find these talents so natural to you that you tend to underrate them. Ask others what they see as your special abilities. They will identify things you don't.

When you have a large pile of blocks (skills) sort them through. Rearrange them into different job structures. Give each combination a name. Call yourself that name: "Doing this, I see I am a designer." "I am a pro-moter." "I am a trainer." "I am a machinist." It is impor-tant to remember you can call yourself any job title you can back up. Employers put names on task clusters (jobs). So can you.

Rearranging your abilities, you build new job op-portunities for yourself. You uncover jobs that, for you, had been hidden.

Strategy No. 5

To create new jobs that fit you, you need to:
REASSEMBLE YOUR SKILLS

You have the ability to do many things you are not aware of. Why not? Because you don't recognize your skills. So you need to list them and appreciate them.

If you try to bring all these up from memory without some reminders, you may find it next to impossible.

To make the process easier, you will find some Memory Joggers in this "Plan". These "Joggers" are not always to be taken literally. Many of them will not apply to you as they stand, but they may start a train of thought which will remind you of other experiences and skills you have had.

To use the Memory Joggers properly:

1. Circle or highlight those items that "ring a bell"...that remind you of your skills and successes. (You will discover that success in anything actually points out a special skill.)

2. Include all your successful experiences, not just those you have been paid for. (Usually these are especially happy experiences.)

3. Make a list of the circled items. After each item, write a sentence or two stating what you did that led to success. Start like this:

> radio: I built a radio that worked well.
> medal: I wrote an essay that won a medal.
> lodge dinners: I planned and supervised dinners for large groups.

4. Don't write: "I was involved." Instead use active verbs ...occupational verbs...such as: "planned, taught, organized, repaired, developed, researched, served, operated, posted."

> Write: "I posted the club dues."
> Not: "I wrote down the dues."

> Write: "I initiated.."
> Not: "I thought up..."

5. Analyze each experience carefully, noticing how your skills and methods tend to appear again and again in the things you have done.

What did you do with information? Did you create it? Research it? Compute it? Analyze it? Coordinate it? Compile it? Copy it? Compare it?

What did you do with people? Advise them? Instruct? Supervise? Entertain? Persuade? Serve? (Or even ignore?)

What did you do with things? Set them up? Operate them? Do precision work? Manipulate them? Build them? Tend them? And what kind of things? (Be specific).

IMPORTANT: A pattern of repetition in your successful experiences points to the kinds of work activities you should look for in a job description.

6. Now you have a supply of skills. These are the building blocks you will use to construct new occupations. Pull these out as you need to fit the employer's job description.

7. When you apply for the job, be sure to emphasize these skills on an extra sheet of paper (employers call these "attached sheets"), or a résumé. This material should accompany the employer's application form.

You may find, once you get into this process, that you liked some things about a specific activity, while you disliked other things. If this occurred on a job, it may be that the part you liked was something you added to the job duties, something not usually considered part of the job description.

Take Ruth, for example.

Ruth was a meat wrapper for a large supermarket. She was very enthusiastic about the work..."enjoyed it immensely," she told me. But lifting the heavy carcasses had strained her back, so now she needed to make a change.

"Did you like cutting and wrapping the meat?" I asked.

Ruth hesitated. "No" she replied. "I really didn't." (Yet this is the principal activity of a meat wrapper.)

"What, then, did you like?" I persisted.

"Oh, I liked talking with all the customers... explaining how to prepare various cuts of meats. I even exchanged recipes with them."

Ruth's enthusiasm showed. It was the public contact aspect she liked...a far cry from cutting and wrapping meat. The job only offered her an opportunity, (the stage, if you like), to do what she really liked to do...give information to customers.

Ask yourself, "Exactly what job duties did I really like?" If you have performed these happily and successfully, then you have identified marketable skills.

Now, just in case you may have overlooked some skills, you will find a list of questions after the Memory

Joggers that will also act as reminders. Consider these carefully, too. The more material you have, the better jobs you will build.

Self analysis is not easy, but when you persist, over the period of a few days, you will build up your confidence and self esteem. If you do this thoughtfully, you will be pleasantly surprised to discover how competent you are.

Here's how to uncover your talents:

First day: START THE FIRST PAGE OF MEMORY
            JOGGERS
(Circle those that "ring a bell".)

Second day: DO THE SECOND PAGE OF
             MEMORY JOGGERS
(Do these remind you of some experiences?)

Third day: THIRD PAGE OF MEMORY
            JOGGERS
(These help to highlight your talents.)

Fourth day: THESE WILL NUDGE YOUR
             MEMORY, TOO:
(and identify your skills.)

Everything you do requires you to perform thinking of some kind, to respond to people or ignore them, and to use things and objects in getting the job done.

The Dictionary of Occupational Titles calls

The thinking you do ....relationship to DATA
The response to others.........relationship to PEOPLE
The working with objects........relationship to
THINGS.

In easier terms, it means we THINK not at all,
somewhat...or a great deal...when we perform an activity.

For example: If we are lying in the sun by the pool,
we probably use our thinking just enough to notice that
we are comfortable, we have used our sunscreen lotion,
and there are no demands on our time until hunger pangs
take over. (Minimal mental activity.)

Or...if we are going out for dinner, we will think about
where we will go, who we will invite to join us, whether
we will dress for dinner, what will we want on the menu,
and perhaps, whether we can afford the price. (Information gathering and analyzing.)

On the other hand, if we are planning to design and
construct a new house, our mental activity will be very
intense and detailed. (Creative planning.)

We RESPOND TO PEOPLE in various ways. We
may ignore them, talk briefly with them, or get deeply
involved in their lives.

For example: At the pool we may ignore them and
take a nap. (Little or no involvement.)

Inviting them to dinner and spending an evening together means a friendly exchange of information. (Some social contact).

Listening to their problems and counseling them requires you to get deeply involved in their lives. (In-depth response.)

Finally, WORKING WITH OBJECTS may not be much....may be a fair amount...or may be heavy involvement.

For example: The novelist is only incidentally involved with his word processor. It is merely a means toward the end of getting ideas down on paper. (Used only as a tool.)

The secretary uses office machines most of the day in putting information and correspondence into usable form. Operation of office machines therefore is a major ingredient of job performance. (Objects are important to job performance.)

The machinist is heavily involved with the use of materials and equipment essential to producing his product. (Objects are the major focus of the job.)

Generally you will find out that...

1. Professional and managerial workers place strong emphasis on the use of DATA. (Ideas and facts.)

2. Technical and clerical workers combine DATA and the use of THINGS in almost equal amounts.

3. Industrial workers customarily are required to deal intensely with EQUIPMENT, MATERIALS, AND MACHINES.

Now begin with the Memory Joggers, starting on the next page.

"KNOW THYSELF"

YOU ARE EMBARKED ON A GREAT ADVENTURE

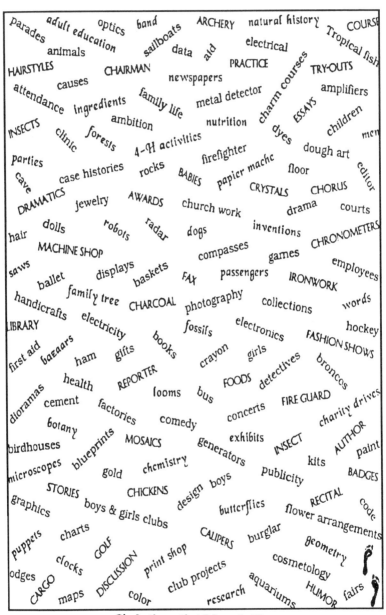

Parades adult education optics band sailboats ARCHERY natural history COURSE
animals data aid electrical Tropical fish
HAIRSTYLES CHAIRMAN PRACTICE TRY-OUTS
causes newspapers charm courses amplifiers
attendance ingredients family life metal detector ESSAYS children
INSECTS ambition nutrition dyes men
clinic forests 4-H activities dough art
parties case histories firefighter floor editor
cave rocks BABIES papier mache CRYSTALS CHORUS
DRAMATICS jewelry AWARDS church work drama courts
hair dolls robots radar dogs inventions CHRONOMETERS
saws MACHINE SHOP compasses games employees
ballet displays baskets FAX passengers IRONWORK
handicrafts family tree CHARCOAL photography collections words
LIBRARY electricity fossils electronics FASHION SHOWS hockey
first aid bazaars ham gifts books crayon girls broncos
diaramas health REPORTER looms bus FOODS detectives charity drives
cement factories comedy concerts FIRE GUARD
botany blueprints MOSAICS exhibits INSECT AUTHOR paint
birdhouses generators kits BADGES
microscopes gold chemistry publicity
STORIES CHICKENS design boys RECITAL code
graphics boys & girls clubs butterflies flower arrangements
puppets charts CALIPERS burglar geometry
clocks GOLF print shop cosmetology
lodges DISCUSSION club projects aquariums HUMOR fairs
CARGO maps color research

Circle those that "ring a bell",...

34

radio
SCRAP BOOKS students crafts LEADERSHIP photographs school bus
brush WILDLIFE target programs ambition piano
impromptu talks kites shrubs ASTRONOMY shop VARIETY SHOWS history
projects cargo politics diesel pictures
LANGUAGES puzzles rubber WEATHER
student government biographies
mistletoe BIBLE STUDIES psychology poetry
technical trial courts LAPIDARY WORK dinner CROSSWORD PUZZLES
jam sessions cases sports team leather laboratories social work
camp soil conservation
handicapped BARBERSHOP teenagers FICTION houses engines
ponds architecture science design cabinet
MAGIC jazz SCIENCE FICTION PUBLIC RELATIONS
repair cameras auctions make-up tiles
records TODDLERS posters EQUIPMENT bench Sunday school AIRPORTS
archaeology reporter arrangements database embroidery criminology
school band signals
tour camp counselor AUTO BODY WORK television
treasurer barbecue keypunch operator law enforcement superstitions
speeches BIOGRAPHIES industrial arts shows tractors
MEDICAL SCIENCES wood novelties gymnastics fire talks
personalities BULLDOZERS BRICK
journalism wallpaper sheetmetal harvest work poles government
telescopes COMMUNITY HEALTH TAXIDERMY school office SPORTS
stamps cafeteria women
AIRPLANES studies agriculture sound building maintenance committee work
yards minerals STATISTICS bicycles math puzzles grinder stunts
theater woodlands TRAVEL totem poles SPIRITUAL cards TELESCOPES
demolition

...to remind you of forgotten experiences,...

35

tree felling invented connected WASHED
NURSING power machining weaving cataloging
upgraded skating inserted campaigning SPRAYING
weighed clamped
HUNTING selling
toy making growing making doll houses CONSOLIDATED COMPETING
SHIPPING landscaping sanding
breeding animals researching POTTERY MAKING sorted
fitted modeling
rug making ROUTING UPHOLSTERING learning
sandblasting scheduling picnicking simplifying classifying
supplied loaded solved
SCORE KEEPING TRAINING DOGS set up maintained
estimated cleaned planning ELECTROPLATING typing
COSTUMING knitting carving riveted dispatching
performed recorded
interior decorating beekeeping watering digging replaced
TRAINING CONTROLLING
MEASURED raked bronco-busting EXAMINED shaping
planting trees carrying problem solving
cartooning counseling painted
conveyed MARCHING inspecting moved
MOUNTAIN CLIMBING meat cutting FOLK DANCING supervised GARDENING
creating wordprocessing scrubbed public speaking
sampling marquetry work expanded
patrolling FASTENED buying explained MOVIE MAKING
TAP DANCING following investigating writing letters cultivating
making renting poured waxed furniture finishing netting
advertising LENS GRINDING PRESSED
blacksmithing debated tended driving
DRILLED diving FORTUNE-TELLING positioned emptied
DUSTED RIGGING

...and to identify your skills.

making lists candlemaking PLUMB directing engraving nurturing READING

running SALESWORK REMODELING clearing brush manufacturing

swimming processing promotion climbing trees WRECKING power skidding

burning operating calculating PUBLISHING soothing

GUIDING TOURS interviewing camping creating disciplining greeting

baking enforcing restoring shaping mining fly tying MEAL PLANING

welding COMPOSING racing DISTILLING reclaiming FRAMING PICTURES fishing

catering grading acting corresponding detecting

polishing rocks silkscreening skating reserving PAVING dressmaking

filing broadcasting DRIVING cooking writing

organizing DISPLAYING tool and die making keyboarding wood burning

HOUSEKEEPING coaching collecting forming teaching

caning building carpentry CASHIERING FINISHING chair caning

walking BOOKBINDING roofing PLAYING GAMES

educating WOODWORKING wrapping cheerleading hiring preserving

policing artistry feather working

cleaning soldering calibrating bench grinding

paint boating EXCAVATING

TANNING computing BUDGETING stoneworking leading camouflage

ranching GLASS BLOWING

blending proofreading CROCHETING flying educating

decorating sewing silversmithing hauling SINGING

NAVIGATING mixing beading

promoting causes escorting drawing

machining DEFENDING dismantling TAILORING transforming mentoring

Have you done or do you want to do any of these?

37

JOB SKILLS ARE OFTEN
HIDDEN IN EVERYDAY ACTIVITIES

1. What do you like to do with your hands?

2. What things or objects do you like to work with?

3. When you read "How to Do It" material, what are you especially interested in learning?

4. When you read for information, what are you reading?

5. When you read for recreation, what are you reading?

6. What kinds of things, or activities do you like to "think up," solve, figure out, create?

7. What do you do successfully with people? Give them information? Carry on a conversation? Advise them? Instruct? Persuade? Supervise? Entertain? Motivate? Serve them?

8. What do you do that you are particularly proud of?

9. What kind of expert would you like to be?

10. What can you do better than your brother or sister or best friend or someone else?

11. Have you ever won a medal? or ribbon? Scout badge? or Brownie points? or gold stars? or a pat on the back? For what?

12. What are you particular about? or fussy about?

13. What projects or problems have you tackled success-fully?

14. What things did you like to do most as a child?

15. What things do you like to do most as an adult?

16. What things do you wish you could have tried? What did you do as a substitute?

17. What makes you especially unique? How are you different from your brother, sister, friends, parents?

18. What have you done that others praised you for?

19. What subjects did you like best in school?

20. As a child, what did you persist in trying to do even though you may not have succeeded?

21. As an adult, what do you keep trying to do although you may not have succeeded yet?

22. What kinds of things are you doing when you "forget the time"?

23. What would you like to be an expert in? What start have you made?

24. What kinds of problems do you like to solve?

technical	artistic
mechanical	design
psychological	health
community	learning
personal relationships	social.

If you have followed instructions carefully from the beginning, you now have two inventories: a job experience inventory, and the Memory Joggers.

Now, be your own career counselor. Start asking yourself these questions: With every activity, you used Data (ideas, information) to some extent, you had some relationship to People, you did something with Things.

How important is data to you? How important is contact with people to you?...and what kind of contact? How important is equipment and what kind of equipment? This begins to describe the form your job should take.

Think each activity through carefully. You will see a pattern of relationships develop.

WHEN THIS PATTERN APPEARS IN THE JOB YOU GET, YOU WILL FEEL HAPPY AND FULFILLED.

40

PLAN NO. 3

FIND A NEED AND FILL IT

Henry Kaiser had a basic formula for success: "Find a need and fill it." By doing exactly that, he founded an industrial empire and made himself a multimillionaire. Even more important, Henry Kaiser created thousands of jobs.

Now you may not want an industrial empire or even a small business, but you can create a job for yourself by means of the same formula.

Why would an employer hire anybody? Generally he is not in the business of dispensing charity, so he must have some other compelling reason. And he has.

Let's think about it.

When you need gas, you drive into a service station. You don't go there just because business is dropping off and the owner needs customers. You go there because he has something you need. He supplies it. You pay him.

Your house needs painting. You hire a painter. When you pay the bill you find a large item marked "labor".

You have, then, actually paid the wages of that painter. But you generally don't pay such charges unless you want something done.

Nor do you go to an attorney because he wants a new car or a trip to the Caribbean. You pay him for something you want done. For a brief time, you have hired an attorney.

In all these cases, you have created a job because you had a need. Temporarily you were the employer.

In the same manner other employers hire because they need something done... not because you need a job. A job is a way of solving a problem. Employers hire because they have problems that need solving:

a) Problems in marketing their products, so they need salesmen and advertising managers.

b) Problems in keeping track of paperwork, so they need bookkeepers and secretaries.

c) Problems in supervising employees, so they hire foremen, team leaders, and directors.

d) Problems in sweeping the floor, so they hire janitors.

e) Problems in meeting deadlines, so they hire planners and organizers.

It is apparent, then, that every job is a problem solving job and THE EMPLOYER HIRES PROBLEM SOLVERS. If you can solve some kind of problem plaguing the employer, you have a job.

Strategy No. 6

Every employer needs help of some kind, so...
BE A PROBLEM-SOLVER

Each activity the employer undertakes creates needs for himself. Some of these needs he takes care of himself. Some he hires others to fill. Some he doesn't have the time to consider at all, so these situations remain unsolved. This is where you come in.

Expansion in a business or industry means business is good, but this expansion creates peripheral needs.

1. Hiring an engineer may create the need for a technician.
2. Hiring a new manager may create need for a confidential secretary.
3. Taking on new employees may create a need for trainers.

All these activities pose new problems. Problems for the employer are potential jobs for somebody. Even closing a business creates needs, although these decline as the closing takes place. With the closing, there is:

43

1. Additional packing and shipping
2. Disposal of inventory and equipment
3. Cleaning and securing the premises
4. Dismissing staff

Think of some work problems you have encountered and how you solved them. Your abilities along these lines are assets to offer an employer.

When the employer says he has no jobs, he is really saying "I don't know how to pay you," or "I don't know how to use you." Rarely does he mean, "The work is all done." Therefore, if you can make money or save money for an employer, this is the "Help Wanted" most employers want.

Think of yourself, then, in the role of a problem solver, not a problem carrier. Problems the employer doesn't need.

Look around you with the eyes of the employer. What work is stacking up? What emergencies are inadequately covered? Where are operations bogging down? Where can you be a definite asset?

It can be something as simple as this: Ellen was making some purchases in a small craft shop operated solely by the owner. In the course of the conversation, she learned that the owner had no time off for lunch and had difficulty getting to the bank during business hours. Ellen offered to come in each day at noon to wait on customers. The owner accepted the offer.

As business picked up, Ellen was hired for half days, and finally the time came when the shop was prosperous enough for a full-time clerk...Ellen, of course. Ellen had found a need and filled it.

And then there was Ed. Ed is a vigorous 60 year old businessman who found retirement not to his liking. Looking around for something to do, he noticed that often the houses belonging to his age group needed re-roofing. He also observed that his peers preferred to do business with the more mature adult rather than the younger salesmen.
.
So Ed approached a major roofing company with his idea. He would sell re-roofing to the older customers. The company agreed to give the idea a try. The idea worked so well that in a short time Ed became the top salesman in the company. He, too, had found a need and filled it.

There are others.

Warren took on evening work as a bookkeeper for a friend's small business. Soon he had so many calls from other small businesses that he quit his regular job and opened his own bookkeeping service.

Roberta offered to act as an on-call teller after waiting in line at an understaffed savings and loan. She soon found other financial institutions had a need for her services when one or more of their tellers was absent.

Judy was a medical technician more interested in the operation of the machines than in patient treatment. When she made this discovery, Judy contacted manufacturers of related equipment suggesting they train her as a service representative. She pointed out the money-saving and time-saving value of her experience which would reduce the cost of training her. The first manufacturer who invited her in for an interview hired her.

Do you have a problem in your daily life that also may be a problem for a number of people in the community? Can you find a solution that is not yet available to everybody? Then you have the seed of a business of your own. It works this way:

Looking for work? (You have plenty of company in this.) Are you buying an armful of papers and searching through pages of ads each day? Can you think of an easier and more efficient way to do this? Reginald Robinson, founder of Ad Finders, Inc., did.

Reginald Robinson wished a computer would do the search for him. He solved the problem by setting up a computer service that searches the classified ads of up to thirty newspapers, and then narrows the search to particular categories. Job seekers pay a fee based on the number of newspapers being searched. Ad Finders, Inc. mails or faxes these ads to the subscribers.

Result? The problem is solved and Reginald Robinson has created his own job.

Are you suffering gridlock getting to work in a major city? So are a lot of others. Daily commuters have a daily problem finding parking space, and then getting from that space to the office.

Kaiser Iqbal thought about it for some time. He came up with a solution: Park and Ride, a variation on the service offered by park and fly lots near airports. From a state owned car lot beneath a freeway, Iqbal's Park and Ride shuttle bus delivers commuters to the city's financial district.

Result? One solution to metropolitan gridlock, and Kaiser Iqbal has created his own job.

There are countless problem-solving jobs out there. With imagination, you, too, can uncover one for yourself.

PLAN NO. 4

ORGANIZE A NETWORK

Job hunting is serious business. If you're the laid off worker, you may have to resist the temptation to become the laid back applicant. Unless you have unlimited resources, you don't have time to take a vacation. Income has ended, but outgo increases.

Locating job opportunities takes time and money. True, you will probably find several suitable openings as time goes by, but you can increase your effectiveness by putting a team to work on your behalf.

Strategy No. 7

SET UP A PERSONAL NETWORK

Several pairs of eyes and ears will generate more job possibilities in a short time than you can alone. So it makes sense to establish your own information network. This network, made up of your associates, will give you access to information you could not obtain by yourself.

To begin with, get rid of the notion that being out of a job is somehow a disgrace. Then you feel freer to approach people for their help. Keep in mind that everybody who now holds a job was once out of a job. You have nothing to feel inferior or disgraced about. It happens to all of us, espccially to politicians, coaches, and corporate presidents.

How do you organize a network?

1 . Make a list of friends, relatives, neighbors, and business acquaintances who might be in a position to learn about openings for your kind of work. These will be your basic information network.

Keep in mind you are going to ask for information. You are NOT going to plead for a job or beg for sympathy. This would dry up your contacts faster than anything else you can do. Further, you are NOT going to ask that your friends recommend you for the job. Let them think of this possibility themselves. What you want at present are tips.

2 . Decide exactly what kind of work you are seeking. After all, it would be absurd to ask others to help you find your kind of job when even you don't know what that job looks like. Write down a clear description of the work you want to do. If you need help, go to the library or the State Employment Service and ask to see the Dictionary of Occupational Titles. In this you will find job descriptions which will help you in preparing one of your own.

3 . Prepare a short list of your own skills and accomplishments which indicate you can do the job. This list

will also help your network to consider related jobs you might be able to perform.

4 . This is your plan of action. You will send a brief friendly letter to each person on your contact list. You will state simply that you are in the process of a job change and would appreciate learning of any suitable openings which come to his or her attention.

In addition to the letter, you will send, on a separate sheet, the description of the kind of work you are seeking and your qualifications to perform this work, (a résumé, if you wish). Ask for tips on this or similar jobs. Emphasize that you are NOT asking the individual to recommend you, only to let you know of possible openings. Stress the fact that you will take the initiative from there.

Make everything as easy for your contacts as possible. Suggest that they save time and effort by jotting down any ideas in the margin of your letter and return it to you. Then enclose a stamped, self-addressed envelope for that purpose.

Offer to check back in a week or two. Thank them for any help they can give. In a postscript to your letter, suggest they keep your résumé at hand in the event something new opens up.

If you have an answering machine, suggest they leave a message on it if that would be easier. Then, don't neglect to call them back.

5. Once the ideas begin coming in, you will expect

to write a short letter of appreciation or make contact by telephone. Let people know that their efforts are helpful.

Strategy No. 8

ADVERTISE FOR IDEAS

When you have your personal network under way, you may want to expand it to include the whole community. You do this by advertising rather than by personal letter. However, avoid the Job Wanted section of the newspaper. These ads are notoriously poor in generating responses. Instead, if you are up to making a bold move, do what John did.

John, a professional job developer, tuned into everybody's network. John tried a display (not classified) ad in a local newspaper offering a small monetary reward for information on a variety of related jobs. (Related jobs are those that have a number of similarities in their requirements.) The reward would be paid to that person who first suggested the opening for which his client was later hired.

This ad with the reward resulted in ten times the number of suggestions during the space of a single week as the same ad without the reward brought in two weeks.

Of course, if you decide to offer a reward, your original network should be told and given the opportunity to participate in the game. A reward is a strong motivational factor impelling individuals to let you know about openings immediately, instead of putting the matter aside for a few days.

Consider first how much the reward will be, how to keep track of the order in which suggestions arrive, and, finally, who will be responsible for picking the winner, assuming more than one person has submitted the suggestion which got you the job.

If you are somewhat reluctant to advertise, think about this: Advertising for ideas does not necessarily mean putting a public notice in the newspaper. A very great part of advertising includes promoting your talents. This is commonly done by sending résumés plus cover letters to the companies for which you want to work.

Keep the material in the résumé focused toward the job you want. The cover letter should highlight specific accomplishments in similar work.

An effective way to get name recognition before executives is to send congratulatory letters about their promotions, appointments, and public appearances when you run across newspaper or television reports. As you send a clipping plus your congratulations, DO NOT MENTION A JOB AT THIS TIME. Keep the content of the message focused on the executive.

At a later time, you may offer productive suggestions concerning the business. At that point you may also offer your services.

Make an effort to learn complimentary things about your prospective employer, his business, and members of his staff. This will start a pattern of name recognition (yours) and will provide a partial answer to the interview question: "Why do you want to work for this company?"

Strategy No. 9

CONTRIBUTE TO A JOB BANK

If you are part of an employment help club, sometimes referred to as a "job club," you have the foundation on which to develop a job bank. For this you need to use a cohesive group. We have already discussed your personal network and the community network. The employment help group is another team you can, indeed should, use to your advantage.

It is common for community colleges and other adult educational schools to schedule classes in job search skills and career choice.

On occasion, business or social organizations sponsor workshops in employment preparation. Many churches and synagogues offer support groups for jobseekers. If you rank as a senior worker, contact your State Employment Service office and Area Agency on Aging for referrals to groups that can help you. Federally funded programs in most communities assist those workers over 55 who meet low income guidelines.

The AARP WORKS program, begun in 1987, offers a series of job search workshops for mature workers in 75 cities to prepare for new employment to meet their needs and abilities.

State Employment Service offices frequently provide meeting places for volunteer self-help groups in the management, professional, and technical fields. Watch for names such as these:

> 40 Plus; Experience Unlimited;
> Pro Match; Alumnae Resources;
> and Career Network Women.
> Ask at your local state office.

Jobs are available in the most unexpected places. Motel 6 is looking for good managers, so they say on their catalog of locations. McDonald's (yes, the hamburger McDonald's) has a program called 'McMasters' that caters to workers over 55.

Whatever the sponsorship, if the group has an employment help project for its members, join it. You will benefit from the moral support the other members give you. You also have the base on which to develop a job bank.

A "job bank," like any other kind of bank, is a place to make deposits and withdrawals. In the case of the job bank, "deposits" consist of information about current job openings. "Withdrawals" come when members make use of the information to apply for jobs.

Where do the deposits come from? There are many openings which come to the attention of the members each week. During the course of a day, you, and others in your group, will read about, hear about, discover, or uncover a variety of job openings.

Do you know of a change coming in a business? Have you learned that the custodian, or the secretary, or the vice president, or the department supervisor is leaving? Did you see a job notice posted on a bulletin board somewhere? Was there a sign hung out at a factory saying "Now hiring: Mechanics, Welders, Assemblers"?

Job tips come from all directions. Did your neighbor tell you over the back fence that his company is expanding? Or did you find out at the local bank that they are looking for a loan officer? All these are valuable tips.

In San Francisco, California, twelve unemployed friends formed their own job cooperative. They offer a wide variety of home and office services. By combining their talents and contacts they assist one another in finding work.

Part of the resources you will bring in may be the information you get from your personal network ... information you can't use, but somebody else might. If you have casually dismissed these opportunities because they do not apply to your needs, remember that many of them have potential for others in your workshop or class. Bring the information in.

The job bank is built as each individual deposits his knowledge of employment opportunities.

To put it another way, at each meeting of the class or workshop, every one has an obligation (an assignment, if you wish) to report to the other members of the group specific jobs he has unearthed on his job-hunting rounds. From this constantly renewed pool of information, then, any participant, including you, may apply for one or more jobs.

The success of the job bank, like any cooperative venture, depends on each member making his contribution, on being willing to share information freely. Freeloading should be firmly dealt with. No deposit. No withdrawal.

Keep a small notebook in your purse or coat pocket to note any jobs you learn about. If you don't have a job search group and are not in a position to form one, make yourself a one-person referral service.

Learn about job openings...all kinds... then phone people you think might be interested either because they are out of work or because they are looking for a change.

This, again, increases your personal network as you encourage them to exchange information with you. Help others to move up or move laterally on the career path. The job they vacate may be one you would like. In any event, you have made a friend.

SUMMARY

You are responsible for the success of your network. The interest and help you offer others, more than anything else, creates in them a desire to help you.

Show an interest in the welfare of each member of your network. Keep a notebook of individuals and their families. Use this information in a friendly conversation when you make contact with them.

Any kindness, encouragement, praise, or thoughtful act expands your contacts because it draws people to you. The help you offer should not be related to job-getting on your part. To do so would taint the kindness.

When the time comes that you do contact any member of your network specifically for job information, get details about the job and about the company.

Following this contact, write a thank-you note. A written expression of appreciation keeps the lines of communication open wide.

The job bank is an excellent resource for specific job openings. As a direct result of the job bank idea, I have seen attendance drop in my classes and workshops. Why? The participants got jobs.

In brief, it is wise to multiply your effectiveness. You will find you have more choices and you will have them earlier in your job search as you use the resources of your connectors...

1. Your personal network;

2. The community network; and

3. A cooperative job bank.

Tom Peters, syndicated columnist, writes: "Connection power... the ability to tap, and then work with, a shifting array of participants for a finite period of time...is perhaps the premiere skill called for in the emerging economy. Oddly enough, it's the connectors, not the so-called 'doers', who usually transform society."

Cultivate your connectors.

PLAN NO. 5

CHECK THE EMPLOYERS' "WANT LIST"

When you have spent some time beating the bushes for a job, it can be comforting to learn that there are employers out there who are beating the bushes looking for you. Some of these searches take the form of corporate recruitment programs.

If your best efforts have netted small game, take heart. How would you like access to hundreds of employers who offer, not a single job, but multiple jobs right now? The College Placement Annual, now called JOB CHOICES, is such a list.

The former College Placement Annual has an honorable record as a resource for those in administration, business, nontechnical career fields, engineering, the sciences, computers, health, medical, and other technical fields.

Although the recruiting annual originally emphasized the search for graduating seniors, in recent years employers have opened job opportunities for applicants with "academic training," associate degrees, advanced degrees, bilingual skills, and applicable job experience. A number of employers offer cooperative programs and summer employment.

Each year corporate employers advertise in JOB CHOICES and send recruiters to colleges and universities throughout the United States. Hiring, however, is not limited to recent college graduates.

To make the most of this potential, you need to sit down and do a thorough job of looking at the information offered. You will find the annual, JOB CHOICES, at college placement offices and libraries. If you live in an area some distance from a college or university, and your library does not carry JOB CHOICES, find out from the reference librarian if you can obtain use of the series through temporary loan from another library. Failing this, you can purchase the JOB CHOICES series from the College Placement Council, Inc., at 62 Highland Avenue, Bethlehem, PA 18017. (Tel. 610-868-1421)

The JOB CHOICES series is divided into four volumes.

Volume I: PLANNING JOB CHOICES, has a wealth of sound advice for the serious jobseeker. This volume is useful, not only to the new graduate, but also to those who have been in the work force for some years. Why? Because it has tips and techniques that update career choices and refine jobseeking skills. After all, getting a job today requires "state of the art" information, too.

It would be foolish to ruin your opportunity for employment because of a horse and buggy approach. Volume I should be read and considered thoughtfully in relation to your own self-marketing methods.

Volume II: JOB CHOICES IN BUSINESS, contains information on employers offering occupations usually classified as non-technical. In addition to the usual administrative and business functions, the creative arts and entertainment functions are included, along with occupations involving education, communication, and information. Still other occupations deal with health services, legal/correctional functions, manufacturing/production, marketing/sales/promotion, scientific/technical, and social services.

Volume III: JOB CHOICES IN SCIENCE AND ENGINEERING, is a catalog of employment opportunities in engineering, science, the computer field, and other technical sciences. This volume reflects the great diversity of anticipated openings for those trained in these specialties.

Volume IV: JOB CHOICES IN HEALTHCARE, offers information from employers hiring in allied health care fields. The Occupational Index Categories in Volume IV are listed as (1) clerical, (2) clinical laboratory services, (3) dentistry, (4) dietetics and nutrition, (5) education, (6) health information and communication, (7) health services administration, (8) medical, (9) nursing, (10) pharmaceutics, (11) psychology, (12) science and engineering, (13) social work, (14) technical instrumentation, (15) therapeutics, (16) veterinary medicine, and (17) vision care.

With health care among the thirty fastest growing occupations in the United States, the possibility of locating a position in the health care field is excellent. JOB CHOICES gives you the information to consider a broad range of employers.

A serious investment of your time to study these volumes is worthwhile. The volumes in the JOB CHOICES series are set up to serve the needs of employers, placement counselors, and applicants, although from differing perspectives. For you, the applicant, each career opportunity book, includes an Employer Index, an Occupational Index, a Geographic Index, and a Special Employment Index.

Volumes II, III, and IV set forth a tantalizing array of job possibilities. You will find that each volume has indexes:

THE EMPLOYER INDEX

This first index merely names the employers who have elected to appear in JOB CHOICES, and the page or pages on which their narratives may be found. If the employer is large enough to have divisions and subsidiaries, these are also listed.

oyer information is the main thrust of the JOB CHOICES series. The major portion of each volume is taken up with detailed factual material on each company. There's a wealth of it.

In general, the employer information supplies: (1) company facts, (2) narrative, (3) opportunities and requirements, (4) career development program, (5) miscellaneous benefits, and (6) how to apply.

1. Company facts: These include the company name, address, and the recruitment coordinator. If the employer has diverse operating units, then the names and addresses of the regional contacts are given. Usually there is a brief statement covering products, services, and activities.

2. Company narrative: This gives the background of the company, company philosophy, and projected future growth and development.

3. Opportunities and requirements: Here are stated the specializations needed, often by company functional areas. For example, the occupations demanded by the design or production departments, or needed by sales industrial marketing. Entry level (trainee) opportunities are itemized with their corresponding disciplines (major studies). Often the need for experienced professionals is included.

Some of the employers include charts and graphs depicting a series of professional disciplines and the department or divisions where they will be needed. These charts are particularly helpful in understanding a number of uses for your skills.

4. Career development program: Companies offer a variety of inducements to applicants. These include:

student summer programs
summer internships
cooperative education programs
mentor programs
on-the-job training
tuition reimbursement programs

In addition, there are promotional ladders and professional advancement processes.

5. Miscellaneous benefits: All of the companies offer major benefits, among which are medical care, retirement benefits, vacation plans, and others.

6. How to apply: There are several career entry points, usually....

(a) direct application
(b) college recruiting
(c) associate development programs
(d) continuing education

The various employers state the degrees they are looking for, such as...

(a) Bachelor's degree
(b) Master's degree
(c) Doctoral degree
(d) MBA (Master's Business Administration).

IMPORTANT: Although the employer narratives state specifically what the employer is seeking, don't allow yourself to be limited by these statements. If you believe that you have good skills which would benefit the company, then apply. Few job requirements are absolute.

THE OCCUPATIONAL INDEX

The Occupational Index lists specific corporate employers by their current occupational interests. This is particularly helpful if you don't know how your skills fit into the world of business and industry.

Strategy No. 10

LEARN WHO IS RECRUITING APPLICANTS WITH YOUR SKILLS

Are you an astrophysicist, a biological oceanographer, a hydrologist, plasma physicist, a transportation engineer, or geologist? Or do you deal in configuration management analysis, job analysis, or geography...or none of these? Whatever your specialty, you will find JOB CHOICES is useful in pointing out specific employers in a great variety of occupational fields.

THE GEOGRAPHICAL INDEX

The Geographical Index is a listing of employers by location. In JOB CHOICES you find information on the functions performed by the corporations at different locations. These functions may be that of corporate headquarters, or production, or research, or sales and distribution, or others. Such information focuses your job search on those organizational functions most likely to require your special talents.

For example, let's take International Paper, one of the world's largest paper companies. You would not be surprised to learn International Paper produces papers and corrugated containers and even lumber and wood products.

International Paper also reports it is involved in oil and gas exploration and drilling. Do you also know it engages in real estate activities? Knowing this, then, if your training was in mining, you would usually not apply for work in one of the other operations. On the other hand, if your education has been in real estate, you might never have thought of International Paper as a possible employer. The Annual can steer you into new as well as in the obvious directions.

Strategy No. 11

USE JOB CHOICES FOR CLUES TO COMPETITIVE INDUSTRIES OR BUSINESSES IN YOUR AREA WHO MIGHT NEED YOUR SKILLS

Next comes the question: "What if the company who uses my training does not have facilities in my area?"

If you are unable to relocate, then consider the competition. At least now you know the type of industry or business which employs your kind of talent. Let's suppose your specialty is in information systems. ABC Company engaged in the development, installation, and operation of information systems may be located in New York and not in your home state. How about applying to a similar company located in your own area?

How can you learn the name of competitive industries?

Of course, refer to the JOB CHOICES ANNUALS for companies in similar fields. Search the Yellow Pages in telephone books for the area where you want to work. Read company ads, brochures, and local newspapers. Ask at your employment office for likely industries and businesses.

Strategy No. 12

FOR OUT OF AREA EMPLOYMENT, CONSULT JOB CHOICES

Would you like to work outside the continental United States? You will find job openings in Alaska, Hawaii, Puerto Rico, Canada, and elsewhere. There are also employers who offer foreign employment to U.S. citizens and to foreign nationals.

Consult the other college recruiting publications .

Check at the library for out-of-area publications carrying employment listings.

Read out-of-area newspapers and regional publications for information.

Read federal job information for positions in other areas.

The JOB CHOICES series is not the only resource. College placement offices and libraries receive a number of similar publications such as..

Career Opportunity Index
The Atlanta JobBank
The Boston JobBank
The Chicago JobBank
The Dallas-Ft.Worth JobBank
The Denver JobBank
The Detroit JobBank
The Florida JobBank
The Greater Chicago JobBank
The Houston JobBank
The Los Angeles JobBank
The Minneapolis-St.Paul JobBank
The New York JobBank
The Northern California JobBank
The Ohio JobBank
The Pennsylvania JobBank
The Philadelphia JobBank
The Phoenix JobBank
The San Francisco Bay Area JobBank
The Seattle JobBank
The Texas JobBank

The Washington D.C. JobBank... and more.

These and other job hunting guides, help you to formulate a target list of possible employers in your field. They tell you who to call, where to write, and give you advice on what to say.

While you are exploring the information at the College Placement Office, find this out:

1. Does the placement office post position openings?

2. Are there openings filed in binders at the tables?

3. Did you look at bulletin boards in this office?

4. Where do they post teaching positions and educational administrative jobs?

5. Does this office publish an employment newsletter? If so, find out how to get a copy.

Strategy No. 13

USE JOB CHOICES TO IDENTIFY EMPLOYERS WHO SEEK YOUR DEGREE (OR LACK OF IT), AND /OR YOUR EXPERIENCE

SPECIAL EMPLOYMENT INDEX

This index furnishes the names of employers having

a particular interest in applicants with work experience, and those with associate and graduate degrees.

Among the unusual categories employers will consider, JOB CHOICES lists: "Associate Degrees, Bilingual Proficiency, Doctoral Degrees, Executive Management Programs, Experienced People, Experiential Education, International Employment offered to Foreign Nationals, International Employment offered to U.S. Citizens, M.A. Degrees, M.B.A. Degrees, M.S. Degrees, Post-Doctoral Degrees.

Perhaps your formal education ended with an associate degree. Don't let the emphasis on advanced degrees discourage you. There is still good news. JOB CHOICES has a healthy listing of companies and organizations who welcome your supportive skills. Keep in mind the engineer needs the technician, the scientist needs research assistants, and every specialist needs help with the practical development of ideas. You may be the answer.

If you have experience in your field, so much the better. There is a long list of employers who would be pleased to get the additional benefits from employing a worker with experience.

Publications similar to JOB CHOICES also offer like information.

Consider a variety of approaches within an organization. Could you work up a career ladder to the position you want?

Learn alternative ways of filling a position. Emphasize your accomplishments on your résumé. Have you had related work experience? Will the employer accept college credits plus volunteer work plus paid experience as completing his requirements?

Look at the employment section of the Standard Periodical Directory. This directory lists more than 60,000 magazines, journals, newsletters, directories, house organs, and association publications. Find the names of those that have employment listings, then look up these particular periodicals for the listings.

Strategy No. 14

USE JOB CHOICES TO LOCATE SPECIFIC OPPORTUNITIES FOR STUDENTS, SUCH AS COOPERATIVE PROGRAMS, INTERNSHIPS, SUMMER EMPLOYMENT

Are you a student interested in working part-time for an employer in your field, and attending school part time? JOB CHOICES lists many employers who are willing to work out such cooperative programs with students.

1. Are you looking for summer employment in your field of study? Check out the employers in JOB CHOICES who offer it.

2. Contact the Financial Aids Office and Student

Placement Office at the college you attend for local opportunities for internships and summer jobs.

3. Write directly to any company asking for the possibility of a program with them. Find out from the recruiting officer what cooperative program would be considered by them.

4. Prepare a prospectus (a plan outlining what you propose to offer). Study the cooperative programs already set up by the college to learn what format of prospectus companies want. Then develop a thorough presentation.

5. Find out if the college has a cooperative program coordinator. If so, this individual is a valuable contact for you.

Strategy No. 15

RESEARCH YOUR POTENTIAL EMPLOYERS THOROUGHLY. FIND SEVERAL NICHES WHERE YOU WILL FIT.

The JOB CHOICES series gives considerable information on companies, but you need to obtain more details.

Send for recruiting material. It is often loaded with ideas on how to enter a company. Do library research with corporate annual reports, business, and technical journals such as Dun and Bradstreet, Standard & Poor's Corporation Records, Thomas' Register of American Manufacturing, Moody's Industrials and other Moody's, and Standard Register of Advertisers.

Read the Catalog of Federal Domestic Assistance for ideas on funding of programs that might open jobs for you.

If your taste runs toward opportunities with the federal government, JOB CHOICES devotes several pages to employment opportunities with various agencies. In spite of curtailing government agency budgets, there is still an impressive number of jobs available.

Don't overlook the attractive, well designed advertisements. The Annual calls these "display listings." Read them. These are not company advertisements to market products and services. These ads have one purpose: To lure good applicants. This means you.

From beginning to end, the JOB CHOICES series is an important resource for those with training in professional, managerial, scientific, engineering, and technical fields.

Each year this annual is distributed to college and university placement offices throughout the United States, and at armed forces installations worldwide. If you cannot obtain your copies from a nearby placement office, write to...

College Placement Council, Inc.
62 Highland Avenue
Bethlehem, Pennsylvania 18017
(Tel: 610-868-1421)

There is a charge for each volume, but the information in JOB CHOICES is an excellent return for your investment.

The JOB CHOICES series is the job applicant's "wish book." Where else could you locate several hundred eager employers all at once?

PLAN NO. 6

GET A FOOT IN THE DOOR

Given a choice, most of us prefer the known quantity to the unknown. Less risk. The known holds no unpleasant surprises. The unknown is a gamble. On this basis, employers tend to promote from within. There are various ways of getting inside.

The Trojan horse demolished the gates. Joshua shouted down the walls of Jericho, and the Assyrians developed a battering ram. In more recent times, the door-to-door salesman applied a strategically planted foot.

All of these methods were successful in opening the door, but none of them were calculated to make friends and influence people. Making friends and influencing employers is what job getting is all about.

It is obvious that the quickest way to get a job in a business or organization is to be inside...to be one of the crew, as it were. Understanding this, you, the energetic job seeker, will look for ways to get a foot in the door.

What's important about this? You want the employer

to see your skills in action. You also need to see the employer in action.

There are other advantages gained from inside. You can learn about jobs in the making. You will detect trends, participate in plans, become acquainted with the philosophy of the business. You will hear of opportunities and avoid pitfalls. You will be surrounded by the management climate...an environment, good or bad, in which you will be required to work.

From the inside, it is easier to learn of changes, of resignations, transfers, terminations, and new openings. Obviously, you will make new friends and thus expand your network.

As you discover what unique opportunities or difficulties are involved, you are in a position to decide whether this company is one with which you want to be affiliated over a long time. You may even learn it would be better to move on early.

The best way to enter any business or organization is to be invited. It is possible to get into the employer's premises by the employer's own invitation.....certainly an improvement over storming the citadel.

To get invited, woo the employer. Here's how to do it.

Try the formal business channels first. These are:

1. temporary work

2. part-time work

3. staff leasing

4. seasonal work

5. cooperative programs and internships

6. volunteer assessment period.

If none of these are available to you, (not because you can't do them, but because the employer does not participate in these activities), then give him an opportunity to discover your talents informally. This requires socializing, by...

1. joining and serving business and professional organizations

2. joining and serving in social organizations

3. attending and participating in conventions and conferences

4. joining the Chamber of Commerce and participating in its committees.

5. sharing a common activity: a sport, a hobby, a community project, the performing arts, a church, etc.

All of these approaches have worked successfully at one time or another for jobseekers. One or more of them can work for you. Let's explore the possibilities.

TEMPORARY HELP AGENCIES

If you are unaware of the advantages of the temporary services, now is the time to find out. You are acquainted with the State Employment Office. You may also know and have used the services of private employment agencies in your job search. These resources helped to locate permanent, full-time jobs. Temporary help agencies supply short-term help (a few days or a few weeks) or part time (a few hours) to employers.

In recent years, the trend among employers is to develop a core of steady employees and then bring in temporaries (short term workers) to supplement this core as needed. As businesses invest in expensive automated equipment and become dependent on it, any idle time represents a loss. Therefore, when a regular operator is absent for any reason, the employer may call in skilled temporaries to help out.

A temporary worker may work for a business for a day, a week, or even several months. As businesses cut their staffs severely or have seasonal growth spurts, they need temporary help to cover the increased work load. But the advantages are not all to the employer.

The two most important aspects of temporary work for you are the possibility of immediate employment (and therefore, income to tide you over), and the opportunity to "sample" a number of business organizations before you apply for a steady job.

As a temporary you have the opportunity to re-enter the work force after a long absence. You have the opportunity for employment if you have not worked before. Temporary assignments give experience and variety.

Working for temporary agencies you have greater freedom to work or not. You have the option to travel, to take time off, to hunt for a more suitable job. Flexible work hours and shortened work days, (sometimes designated "mother hours" because so many women with school age children prefer this arrangement) can be part of your contract.

Occasionally, especially with the major temporary help agencies, such as Manpower and Kelly, you will have the advantage of referral and placement overseas wherever these agencies have offices. Usually this privilege is available only after an extended period of proven service in their employ here in the United States.

There are many temporary help agencies. You will find them listed in the yellow pages of your local telephone book, usually under Employment—Temporary. Quite often they are sister organizations of private employment agencies. Because these two services have very different ways of operating, your relationship with each of them will differ. It is important to understand what to expect.

The private employment agency operates like any other agent. Under contract with you, the agency will search for a job for you. If, as a result of their efforts, you are hired, then you will pay a fee for the service.

A temporary help agency, on the other hand, becomes your employer. The "temporary" hires you, sends you out to do a job, and pays you. You are not hired by the business or organization to which the agency sends you. You remain an agency employee. You will be paid by the agency which then bills the business clients at rates to cover your wages plus agency administrative costs.

To begin with, the pay usually is low, pegged to entry level rates for comparable skills. As these skills improve or the demand for your abilities increases, it is possible to get increased pay. Some temporary agencies, principally the well-established major agencies, are beginning to provide health and life insurance, sometimes paid holidays to long-term employees, and other fringe benefits. Because of the demand for workers with computer skills, more and more temporary agencies train promising employees and pay higher scales for their work.

Most agencies test employees before sending them out. Since the survival of any agency depends upon its ability to please client businesses, this skill testing is understandable.

With the temporary agency as your employer, you are sent to various businesses to help out on a short-term basis. If the business to which you are sent wants to hire you permanently as one of the core staff, then it has an obligation to pay a fee to the temporary agency. After all, the company has lured away a good employee. (This obligation is handled under the contract between the temporary agency and the company which is an agency client.) So, consider the temporary agencies.

What kinds of jobs do the temporary help agencies fill? Most of these agencies supply high demand supportive fields. Generally the jobs are in:

OFFICE SERVICES

Accounting and Bookkeeping
Banking and Cashiering
Data Processing
General Office
Inventory
Office Machines
Records Management
Secretarial and Stenographic
Transcription
Typing
Word Processing

INDUSTRIAL SERVICES

Driving
Labor and Assembly
Light Industrial Services
Machine Trades

Structural and Benchwork Trades
Warehousing and Stock Work

MARKETING

Trade Shows and Seminars
Demonstrations and Sales
Surveys
Merchandising
Auditing

TECHNICAL SERVICES

Designing
Drafting
Engineering
Engineering Support

HEALTH CARE SERVICES

Dental
Medical-Clerical
Housekeeping
Nursing
Emergency Care
Therapy
Laundry
Dietary Work

FOOD SERVICE

JANITORIAL SERVICES

PROFESSIONAL SERVICES

Because of the fluid nature of the national work force, temporary work has lost much of its stigma. More and more professionals in the job market, accountants, data processors, bankers, and even specialists in advertising and marketing, are accepting temporary positions using their professional skills.

Some temporary help agencies are highly specialized, confining their referrals to professional fields such as dental and medical. Others are oriented toward clients who need engineers, designers, or workers in industrial and power maintenance. If your training is specialized, these agencies are worth exploring.

If you decide to try temporary work, take a list of your successful activities with you to the temporary employment agency. This will give the interviewer a better idea of the range of your skills.

When you sign up, be prepared to suggest a number of things you can do. This will broaden the range of job search and help the interviewer to help you.

It is important, if you are going to try working as a temporary employee, to keep in mind the reason you are doing this:

1. to learn about the company
2. to hear first-hand about job openings and
3. to show the employer what you have to offer

As a temporary worker, you may be called upon to work bad hours or an irregular schedule. On the other hand, you may be introduced to new occupations which you have not considered for yourself.

To repeat: the two most important aspects of temporary work for you are the possibility of immediate employment (and therefore income to tide you over), and the opportunity to "sample" a number of business organizations before you apply for a steady job.

Remembering this, you will be less reluctant to accept an assignment which may not be something you want permanently. Temporarily, the job may serve your purposes well

Your goal, then, is not the job, but the opportunity to get through the gate.

Strategy No.17

GET IN LINE FOR A FULL-TIME JOB
BY WORKING PART-TIME

If your financial situation is such that you can survive with part-time work, then this alternative holds possibilities for getting a permanent, full-time job. Part-time work is one side of the coin. Temporary work is the other.

Part-time work usually means short hours each day

and a short work week over an extended period. Temporary work by contrast is often full-time, but for a limited stay. Part-time work customarily means one employer. Temporary work, on the other hand, usually involves several employers.

Working part-time you may be assigned to peak hours when extra help is needed. You may be on call for vacation relief or to replace an employee absent for other reasons.

Part-time work has drawbacks. It tends to command less pay per hour than comparable full-time work, and usually there are no benefits. When there is a severe shortage of workers whose skills are in demand, sometimes a skilled part-time worker is paid more per hour than the regular full-time worker in a similar position. This is a form of compensation some organizations offer for the inconvenience of patchwork part-time employment.

In addition, if business hits a slump, naturally there is no need for the part-time employee who will be the first to go. Nevertheless, part-time work does have the advantage of offering a showcase for your skills and a method of getting into the business or organization.

PART-TIME

How do you get a part-time job? Since it is assumed that you will want to stay with the company where you will work, then the best procedure is to make direct application to that company.

Failing this, the state employment service (free) or a private employment agency (fee) have calls for part-time workers. If you have access to a college placement office, you will find listings of part-time jobs there. Check these sources. Of course, you always have recourse to all the previous strategies we have discussed. These strategies are applicable to part-time as well as permanent full-time jobs.

Over a period of time, you, the part-time worker, become accepted as one of the staff. When a position opens in your line of work, you have already proven yourself. You already know the business procedures. You have worked cooperatively with the regular staff. This means the employer is more likely to hire you permanently than to advertise the position and look elsewhere.

Part-time work (contrasted with temporary work) means less than full-time. It may mean permanent work, but less than eight hours each day. If you need full-time work, consider two half-time jobs with different employers (or even the same employer) for the present. Again, look for a way within the company for greater use of your skills.

Strategy No. 18

EXPLORE THE POSSIBILITIES OF WORKING FOR A STAFF LEASING COMPANY

Recently a new phenomenon has developed in the field of personnel management: staff leasing. The concept is not new. Small businesses have commonly contracted bookkeeping and janitorial services. From this has evolved the contracting of all services. Originally the concept was confined to small businesses. Now even the giants are testing the feasibility of staff leasing. More and more find it fills a unique position in their staffing activities.

When a professional first retains a staff leasing service, it is usual for him to release his current staff. The leasing service then hires this staff which the doctor, dentist, lawyer, or other professional leases back.

Staff leasing is the outcome of the need, particularly in professional offices (doctors, dentists, lawyers, engineers, architects, etc.) to be free from handling personnel problems.

Originally clerical and technical support workers were the leased staff, but now 35% of leased employees are professional and technical.

Leasing frees the professional employer to devote his day to the practice of his profession relieved of paperwork and the difficulties of employee relationships. The staff leasing company takes over staff maintenance such as personnel problems, employee records, insurance, Social Security payment, workmen's compensation, and other deductions. It furnishes benefits not usually affordable for a small business.

The leasing company collects money for salaries plus its administrative fees from the small businessman or professional, computes necessary taxes and deductions, and issues employee paychecks. Employee relationships are handled by the staff leasing company, as are hiring and the removal of employees. "Leased" employees report that they like the mediating role played by the leasing company.

Staff leasing affords a unique way of locating work in professional offices and small businesses. Since it was developed primarily as a service for employers, you will find the leasing companies in the yellow pages of the telephone book under the heading: "Personnel Consultants" or sometimes "Employment Contractors".

Find out from the leasing company what they are looking for to fill their needs. Prepare yourself for these opportunities. Hone your skills. Return to adult school for any classes which will bring you up to date. You can attend days or evenings.

Find out from the agency or staff leasing company of your choice when the selection process begins, and what information they want from you. Then don't delay. Nero could fiddle while Rome burned, but if you procrastinate, you will find yourself on the outside looking in.

Strategy No. 19

USE SEASONAL JOBS AS AN ENTRY

Seasonal work, regardless of the time of the year, is a valid way to get inside a business or organization where you will have access to permanent, full-time opportunities.

Your local state employment office should be able to tell you the kinds of industries which have strong activity in any given month. These industries are likely to require additional workers during such periods, but seasonality patterns of industries vary greatly among states and localities.

The state employment office should have seasonality charts for your specific area. By consulting these, you can plan to apply for seasonal work from one month to six months in advance of the anticipated increase in work force. The employment office will advise you as to the proper time based on previous job orders and local hiring practices.

The state employment division routinely compiles information on industries that use seasonal workers. To do this, the labor market information specialists consider the economic factors, weather conditions, harvest patterns, and governmental projects that require seasonal workers. You can do the same. By knowing the types of industries, such as recreation, hotel, harvesting, processing, etc., you can now locate the employers for yourself. Contact them.

If you ultimately want full-time work, then you will be selective in where you apply for seasonal work. Try to apply for work experience in a field that will contribute to your permanent employment.

Summer work is usually considered the province of students who are out of school and looking toward the next year's tuition costs. This is a justifiable concept, but if we regard summer work as just one of a range of seasonal jobs, then these opportunities become available to everybody.

For summer job directories, see your library, bookstore, or college student placement office. An excellent directory is the annual **Summer Employment Directory of the United States** (published by Writer's Digest Books, 9933 Alliance Road, Cincinnati, Ohio 45242). This directory gives specifics for each state as listed under "resorts, camps, amusement parks, hotels, national parks, businesses, conference and training centers, ranches, restaurants, and the government."

There are other fine summer job directories which supply specific information for stated geographical areas. Again, your library, a bookstore, or the student placement office should have them.

For work more closely related to the area of your training or studies, consult the CPC's **Job Choices Series** (College Placement Council) discussed in Plan 5. In the annual series are listed employers who offer summer jobs with their companies.

Using the CPC's **Job Choices,** write the recruitment officer of the company or companies which appeal to you. Ask for information on summer jobs.

The great secret in getting a summer job where you want it is applying early...as much as six months early. This is especially true of governmental agencies. If you wait until March to apply for a summer job, you can find yourself already three months late. Recruiting for these positions is often completed in January.

Strategy No. 20:

IF YOU ARE A STUDENT, APPLY FOR A COOPERATIVE EDUCATION PROGRAM IN THE FIELD OF YOUR STUDIES

Cooperative education programs again illustrate the foot in the door process. Under these work/study projects, (usually offered to graduates as well as undergraduates) the student contracts to work on either an alternating schedule or a parallel schedule with the cooperating employer.

On the alternating schedule, the student goes to class full-time for a term, then works full-time the next term with his employer. On a parallel arrangement, the student works half days at the employer's place of business and attends classes during the other half.

By the end of the program the student has acquired practical work experience in the field of his studies. He has put theory into practice. In addition, since many employers participating in the program regard it as a recruiting source, often the student who performs satisfactorily is offered a career position.

For information on a number of cooperating employers, check with the CPC's Job Choices series and the student placement office of your college or university.

INTERNSHIPS

To a lesser degree, the internship programs operate somewhat like the cooperative education programs. Under an internship, the student is assigned, as part of his study requirements, a fixed program with an outside agency or business. The work is prescribed by the academic department and the experience covers one term only.

Where the cooperative education student will be paid a small salary, the intern usually receives no pay since his work assignment is actually a class assignment. However, there still remains the opportunity to observe the functions of a business or organization and learn about job openings.

For cooperative education or internships, make direct application. Check with your library for directories of internships which list hundreds of on-the-job training opportunities for all types of careers.

It is also possible to start with a job and turn it into an internship by arrangement with the employer and the college from which you want credit.

Strategy No. 21

VOLUNTEER YOUR PRESENT SKILLS.
VOLUNTEER TRAINING TIME.
EITHER OR BOTH MAY OPEN THE DOOR.

In this era of tight budgets, strong competition, and short profit margins, the wary personnel director or small business manager is reluctant to commit the company to more staff. However there are few who can resist voluntary help, provided it offers the possibility of serving some useful capacity for the company.

This suggests that you provide your own wedge.

Offer to prove your usefulness and skills to the employer free for a limited period of time...say, a week or two. The idea is so seldom broached that you may meet with skepticism. But if you are sincere in your wish to work for a particular company, and if you have given the employer a good indication of what you can do for him, there is a chance that he will take you on, provided this does not bring him into conflict with labor laws and liability exposures

More frequently employers are accepting volunteer work as work experience provided the duties performed are comparable to those required in a similar job under paid employment.

Volunteer your skills for a trial period with an employer, if he feels he cannot afford more help. (This puts you in a position for first consideration for an opening.)

If your skills don't quite meet the need, volunteer your time during a training period with the employer. (Training time is expensive for the employer. If a new employee is hired, his wages or salary exceed his worth for the present. In addition, the productivity of the supervisor or trainer falls because his time is interrupted while he trains the new employee.)

If you need to get applicable work experience, volunteer not just hours but specific skills, such as: audio engineer, animal habitat assistant, designer, medical aide, public affairs director, welder, case aide, book pricer, carpenter, graphics assistant.

Is there a volunteer coordinator in your community? Ask at the employment service or any social agency. Find out where you can get experience in community service in exchange for volunteering.

Offer your specific skills in the arts and sciences, in child care agencies, convalescent homes, the criminal justice system, hospitals, neighborhood centers, switchboards, volunteer agencies, and community activities. You might try the Chamber of Commerce where you will be in contact with business representatives.

As I talked with the personnel director of one savings and loan company, he complained about the lack of substitute tellers.

"Why doesn't someone come in and offer to work for a week free while we train her?" he asked. "If she does a good job, we could use her frequently as an on-call teller. When we get a sick call during rush times, she could almost name her own price."

It's an idea.

Strategy No. 22

WIN FRIENDS TO INFLUENCE PEOPLE.

Up to this point we have talked about getting to know the employer and the employer getting to know you on his home ground where the employer/employee relationship is preserved. These are the formal business channels.

The informal channels are meant to develop friendly relationships with influential representatives of the company. These can be supervisors, foremen, office managers, salesmen, buyers, anybody who knows the company well. Again, the purpose is to learn about job openings.

Even if you are not a joiner, this is the time joining may pay off. Join a business organization. The Chamber of Commerce would be a good start. Join a professional organization in your field of work. Go to meetings. Attend dinners. Accept committee assignments. Work hard on the committee. Shared responsibilities bring a group into shared communication.

Get involved in the publication of a Chamber of Commerce newsletter. There is nothing like a newsletter to bring you into contact with infuential people. You will report events, interview the movers and shakers, and, in the process, they will get to know you.

Help social organizations. Participate in fund raising, community improvement projects, community events. Prominent company representatives frequently chair these committees.

Attend business and professional conferences and conventions in the field of your specialty. Take part in seminars...an active part. Speak up, offer ideas, suggest solutions. There are leaders and thinkers in the audience.

Are your hobbies those of the individuals you want to meet? If so, find a way to share with them, or, take up their interests. Participate in sports, recreation, charity drives, church activities. In short, be visible.

Employers will pass up an applicant with high skills and an abrasive attitude for the applicant with lesser skills and a warm personality. If you are going to work with people you must get along well with people.

Lead where you can. Help where you can. Praise where you can. Someone will see you, like you, and help you on toward getting a job. Friendliness pays off.

Whenever and wherever you put a foot in the door, be sure it's your best foot.

PLAN NO. 7

APPLY WHERE THE EMPLOYER LOOKS

Once you're out of a job, you're soon out of time, too. The bills arrive on schedule. The income doesn't. That's why it's essential to find shorter and more promising routes back to work.

One of these shorter and more promising routes is knowing how personnel executives choose to look for new employees. This is rarely considered seriously. It should be.

The state of Oregon made a survey of methods employers prefer when looking for new employees. An earlier report issued by the U.S. Department of Labor provided information on the methods job applicants found most productive. The strong correlation between successful methods in both studies suggests *it is smart to be where the employer looks.*

There is no standard method for locating applicants. The employer's method varies according to the occupation to be filled and the industry to which the employer belongs. There are, however, certain preferences which can be roughly classified by industry. If you are unaware of these patterns, you may be wasting time and money applying the wrong way. Your search becomes fruitless. What's more, your courage and confidence begin to wane with each futile attempt.

You may come to think that unemployment is your fault...something's wrong with you. Actually the problem may be that you are merely applying incorrectly. By changing the focus of your efforts, you could see marked improvement in your success rate ...even get the job you want.

In the Oregon report, employment and personnel managers rated their preferences among several recruiting methods. These methods were:

(a) OPEN DOOR

Sometimes it's called "Open Door", sometimes it's called "Gate Hires", but either way, this means the employer will accept direct application. Many employers like to have job applicants apply directly even though there may be no openings in the business at the time. These employers then collect a pool of acceptable applicants from which they draw as the need for a new employee arises.

If you apply and the letter in response says something like this: "We will keep your application in our files for consideration at a later date," what the employer is really saying is, "We collect applications from good applicants. When we have an opening, we expect to make a selection from this pool." You have a chance.

If you have ever received a job offer six months after application, this indicates that you were put into the employer's applicant pool. Finally, you have landed on top.

Direct application does not necessarily mean you must go to the office to apply, although this is the common practice among clerical and industrial workers. For professional, managerial, and technical fields, however, the application is frequently made through a résumé introduced by a cover letter, in short, by mail.

(b) ADVERTISING

The employer's advertisement may be as simple as a sign hung in the door of his business or a classified ad in the local newspaper. Or he may purchase advertising in trade, professional, business journals, in college recruiting publications, or in industry newsletters. He may even develop elaborate brochures to be distributed at conventions or conferences or mailed to employment agencies of various kinds.

(c) PRIVATE AGENCIES

Some employers prefer to have outside placement people do the early screening for skills, training, and experience. A private agency which specializes in a particular field, such as medical or industrial, is more likely to have immediate access to qualified applicants. To use these resources, you must file with an agency. When you are placed in a job through agency efforts, you will be charged for their services.

Executive recruiters, an even more elite form of employee search, are retained by employers to find highly competent professionals. The professionals with rare skills in great demand are sought out because they are already successfully employed and proving their value. The employer client, through the executive recruiter, sets about to locate and lure the much coveted worker away from his present job.

Because of the nature of the executive recruiter's work, he does not, as a rule accept applications. Unless you are currently employed in the field of your expertise, unless your competencies are in high demand and low supply, there is little chance that you will be wooed by the "head hunters"...the executive recruiters.

(d) STATE EMPLOYMENT SERVICES

This resource is more frequently used to obtain clerical and industrial workers. It is less productive for those in the professional, managerial, and skilled technical fields. If your capabilities lie in professional, managerial, or technical fields, ask at your local employment service office what assistance is available to those in these occupations.

Some offices, in cooperation with employers, have set up a volunteer task force for this purpose.

(e) SCHOOL/COLLEGE PLACEMENT OFFICE

Because most of these placement offices restrict their services to students, graduating seniors, and those who are obtaining advanced degrees, the employer who uses this contact is often seeking trained entry level employees. Here you must qualify for the services of the college or school placement office in order to be included in the employer's recruiting schedule. Job referrals may also be made by instructors.

(f) TRADE ASSOCIATIONS, PROFESSIONAL ORGANIZATIONS, UNION HIRING HALL

Each of these resources offers employment information to members only. For this reason, to qualify for their services, you must join. If the business or industry in which you want to work uses these sources to get employees, then you should consider making the investment.

The Oregon study, though limited to 140 employers in the Portland metropolitan area, represents the responses from small businesses with less than 500 workers as well as those organizations with more than 1000. Industry groups included manufacturing, finance and insurance, trade, service industries, transportation, construction, and government.

How do employers prefer to get their employees? Here are the results of the study:

FINANCE AND INSURANCE COMPANIES

(Banks, trust companies, credit agencies other than banks, holding companies, dealers in securities, insurance carriers of all types of insurance, their agents and brokers.)

These look for **Professional, Managerial, Technical** staff:

1st: by advertising
  2nd: through application
   3rd: through private agencies
    4th through state employment service
     5th: through college placement offices
      6th: through professional organizations

These look for **Clerical** (Office) employees:

1st: through direct application
  2nd: through state employment service
   3rd: through advertising
    4th: through private agencies
     5th: through college placement offices
      6th: through professional organizations

These look for **Sales** people:

1st: through private agencies
  2nd: by advertising
   3rd: through state employment service
    4th: through college placement
    5th: through direct application
     6th: through trade or professional organizations

These look for **Crafts** workers:

1st: by advertising
  2nd: through state employment service

3rd: through direct application
4th: through private agencies
5th: through union hall
6th: through school placement offices

These look for **Semiskilled** workers:

1st: through advertising
2nd: through state employment service
3rd: by direct application
4th: through private agencies
5th: through school placement offices
6th: through trade association or unions

MANUFACTURERS

(Plants, factories, or mills which characteristically use power driven machines and materials handling equipment. The materials include products of agriculture, forestry, fishing, mining, and quarrying.)

These look for **Professional, Managerial, Technical** staff:

1st: by advertising
2nd: through private agencies
3rd: by direct application
4th: through state employment service
5th: through college placement offices
6th: through professional organizations

These look for **Clerical** (Office) employees:

1st: through state employment service
2nd: through direct application
3rd: by advertising
4th: through private employment agencies
5th: through school placement offices
6th: through trade association or union

These look for **Sales** people:

1st: by advertising
2nd: through state employment service
3rd: by direct application
4th: through private agencies
5th: through school placement offices
6th: through trade associations

These look for **Crafts** workers:

1st: through direct application
2nd: by advertising
3rd: through state employment office
4th: through trade association or union
5th: through private employment agencies
6th: through school placement offices

These look for **Semiskilled** workers:

1st: through direct application
2nd: through state employment service
3rd: by advertising
4th: through trade association or union
5th: through private agencies

6th: through school placement offices

GOVERNMENT

(All federal, state, local, and international government activities, such as the legislative, judicial, and administrative functions, as well as government owned and operated business enterprises.)

These look for **Professional, Managerial, Technical** staff:

1st: through direct application
2nd: through state employment service
3rd: through college placement offices
4th: through professional organizations

These look for **Clerical** (Office) employees:

1st: through state employment service
2nd: through direct application
3rd: through school or college placement offices
4th: by advertising

These look for **Crafts** workers:

1st: through trade association or union
2nd: through direct application
3rd: through private employment agencies
4th: through school placement offices
5th: by advertising

These look for **Semiskilled** workers:

1st: through direct application
2nd: through state employment service
3rd: through private employment agencies
4th: by advertising
5th: through trade association or union
6th: through state employment service

SERVICE INDUSTRIES

(Hotels and other lodging places; establishments providing personal, business, repair, and amusement services; medical, legal, engineering, and other professional services; education institutions; and other miscellaneous services.)

These look for **Professional, Managerial, Technical** staff:

1st: through direct application
2nd: by advertising
3rd: through private employment agencies
4th: through state employment service
5th: through professional organizations
6th: through college placement offices

These look for **Clerical** (Office) employees:

1st: through direct application
2nd: through state employment service
3rd: by advertising

4th: through private agencies
5th: through school placement offices
6th: through trade association or union

These look for **Sales** people:

1st: through direct application
2nd: through state employment service
3rd: by advertising
4th: through trade association
5th: through private agencies
6th: through college placement offices

These look for **Crafts** workers:

1st: through direct application
2nd: through state employment service
3rd: by advertising
4th: through trade association or union
5th: through private agencies
6th: through college placement offices

These look for **Semiskilled** workers:

1st: through direct application
2nd: through state employment service
3rd: by advertising
4th: through school placement offices
5th: through private agencies
6th: through trade association or union

TRANSPORTATION INDUSTRIES

(Enterprises engaged in passenger and freight transportation by railway, highway, water, or air; or furnishing services related to transportation.)

These look for **Professional, Managerial, Technical** staff:

1st: through direct application
2nd: by advertising
3rd: through college placement offices
4th: through professional organizations
5th: through state employment service
6th: through private agencies

These look for **Clerical** (Office) employees:

1st: through state employment service
2nd: through direct application
3rd: through private agencies
4th: through school placement offices
5th: by advertising
6th: through trade association or union

These look for **Sales** people:

1st: through direct application
2nd: through school or college placement offices
3rd: through private agencies
4th: through state employment service
5th: by advertising
6th: through trade association

These look for **Crafts** workers:

1st: through direct application
2nd: through state employment service
3rd: by advertising
4th: through trade association or union
5th: through private agencies
6th: through school placement offices

These look for **Semiskilled** workers:

1st: through direct application
2nd: through state employment service
3rd: through trade association or union
4th: through school placement offices
5th: by advertising
6th: through private agencies

CONSTRUCTION INDUSTRIES

(Generally the construction of dwellings, office buildings, stores, farm buildings, highways, streets, bridges, railroads, tunnels, docks and piers, dams, storm sewers, water projects, airfields, and other projects.)

These look for **Professional, Managerial, Technical** staff:

1st: through private agencies
2nd: through college placement offices
3rd: by advertising
4th: through state employment service

5th: through trade association or union
6th: through direct application

These look for **Clerical** (Office) employees:

1st: through private agencies
  2nd: by advertising
    3rd: through state employment service
      4th: through direct application
        5th: through school placement offices
          6th: through trade association or union

These look for **Sales** people:

1st: through private agencies
  2nd: by advertising
    3rd: through state employment service
      4th: through college placement offices
        5th: through direct application
          6th: through trade association

These look for **Crafts** workers:

1st: through trade association or union
  2nd: by advertising
    3rd: through state employment service
      4th: through private employment agencies
        5th: through direct application
          6th: through school placement offices

These look for **Semiskilled** workers:

1st: through trade association or union

2nd: through direct application
3rd: by advertising
4th: through state employment service
5th: through private agencies
6th: through school placement office

WHOLESALE AND RETAIL
TRADE BUSINESSES

(Organizations whose activities consist of selling goods to trading establishments, or to industrial, commercial, institutions, and professional users. Others sell merchandise for personal, household, or farm consumption.)

These look for **Professional, Managerial, Technical** staff:

1st: by advertising
2nd: through college placement offices
3rd: through direct application
4th: through private agencies
5th: through state employment service
6th: through professional organizations

These look for **Clerical** (Office) employees:

1st: through direct application
2nd: through private agencies
3rd: through state employment service
4th: by advertising
5th: through school placement offices
6th: through trade association or union

111

These look for **Sales** people:

1st: through direct application
2nd: through private agencies
3rd: by advertising
4th: through college placement offices
5th: through state employment service
6th: through trade association

These look for **Crafts** workers:

1st: through direct application
2nd: through state employment service
3rd: by advertising
4th: through unions
5th: through private agencies
6th: through school placement offices

These look for **Semiskilled** workers:

1st: through direct application
2nd: through state employment service
3rd: by advertising
4th: through unions
5th: through school placement offices
6th: through private agencies

Finally, it is not at all uncommon for a single large organization to have several channels through which various occupations are hired. For example, a community college may have a personnel director who is responsible for locating and screening clerical and maintenance workers. The dean of instruction and department chairmen hire

112

instructors. Managers may be channeled through the president's office, and part time instructors for community education outreach centers are frequently selected by the director of each outlying facility.

If you have a question about which channel you should use in a multi-faceted industry, phone the personnel office. Ask for the information you need.

Successful job search requires a well planned strategy. And a correct understanding of where employers look is an essential part of that strategy.

Strategy No. 23

USE THE CHANNEL
THE EMPLOYER PREFERS

If you were looking for buried treasure, you wouldn't grab your spade and start digging just anywhere. You would dig where the treasure is most likely to be.

Apply where the employer is most likely to look for someone with your skills.

PLAN NO. 8

SEARCH THE LIBRARY

We all expect to find tales of romance and adventure in the library, or information on how to build a house or raise orchids, or convert to the metric measurement. However, job seekers rarely consider the library as a help in getting a job.

Get a job through the library? Ridiculous, you think. Yet your community library can be a rich mine of prospective job opportunities.

To begin with, you have the racks and racks of daily newspapers, local and national. If you are geographically mobile, the full range offers wide possibilities for jobs through the classified ads, display ads, and business reports.

If your search must necessarily be limited to your commute range, you still have free access to newspapers within that radius. Pick out the newspapers serving adjacent communities. Read them carefully for opportunities. The job you seek may be advertised in one of these.

You can understand reading the Help Wanted section, but why read the business pages? If you are out of work or expect to make a change, sometimes the employment world seems like a lopsided game of hide and seek. The employers hide. You seek. More often, it's a game of musical chairs. Somebody leaves his job. You watch for the vacancy, and slide in.

Every so often the game changes. Then the employer scrambles to locate you. These are signs that the game is changing:

1. The business announces expansion plans.

2. A new business is moving into your area.

3. The company is promoting a major new product.

4. Government regulations are imposing a new or expanded requirement.

5. There is a merger. The company you're interested in remains the dominant partner.

6. The company receives a major contract, especially if a fixed time limit is part of the agreement

7. Somebody is promoted in the company. Promotions and retirements leave vacancies behind them. Vacancies are job openings.

8. New industry sites are purchased.

When one or more of these conditions exists, the company starts a recruiting campaign. Just how this search for good employees is conducted depends upon the number needed and the kinds of positions to be filled.

At the library you will also find rows of telephone books, each with the ubiquitous yellow pages listing page after page of businesses. By considering the businesses which normally use your kinds of skills, you have a large number of possible employers. (Remember? You don't need to wait for a formal job announcement. You can apply directly to most employers. "Gate hires", we called them.)

Let me illustrate: Dorothy has just finished her training in the use of industrial sewing machines. Now she is ready for a job. Her library can help. Looking in the yellow pages of the phone book under the types of industry where such workers are found, she can expand her potential employer list into as many communities as she likes.

She will find her prospective employers under such headings as: Upholsterers, Furniture Manufacturers, Apparel and Garment Manufacturers, Glove and Mitten Manufacturers, Hosiery Manufacturers, Surgical Appliances Manufacturers, Umbrella Manufacturers, Mattress and Bedding Manufacturers, Drapery Manufacturers, Motor Vehicle and Equipment Manufacturers, Leather Products, Textiles, Textile Bags, Toys and Games, Garment Lettering, and Theatrical Costuming.

Although the telephone books are a good resource for locating potential employers, there are others. In the library, you will find Chamber of Commerce directories, industry directories, directories of manufacturers and wholesalers, and federal and state career directories.

Read trade magazines, utility publications, college newspapers. Don't overlook business weeklies, regional sections of the Wall Street Journal, and display ads for job openings scattered throughout Sunday editions.

If a summer job is your goal, there are publications (usually books) listing kinds of jobs and the employers who offer these. Often the listings give processes for application, including the proper time of year to apply, the names of specific employers, job requirements, addresses and telephone numbers.

In the magazine section you will find periodicals in the fields of your training and experience. Often jobs are listed in the classified section of these magazines. For example, in a recent edition of a publication serving farmers and stockmen, there appeared a display ad from a major seed company offering a professional position to applicants experienced in vegetable crop production.

Strategy No. 24

MAKE A FRIEND OF YOUR REFERENCE LIBRARIAN

If you need help, ask the reference librarian. She is acquainted with the materials and can assist you in locating many things you would not find by yourself.

Use the library's computers, microfiche, catalogs, indexes, bibliographies, directories, guides, and such, especially in the areas of government and business. If these high tech processes are daunting, ask the librarian to show you how to use them.

Maybe you are interested in a government job, city, county, state, or federal. Any of these will probably require you to take civil service tests. Does the prospect upset you? Then ask the librarian for appropriate civil service test books. These manuals teach you the most effective way to take the tests.

But...DON'T WAIT UNTIL THE NIGHT BEFORE THE EXAM TO STUDY FOR IT. Start a month before the scheduled date. Practice the examinations in the test book. Pay attention to the useful hints. These come in handy when you need to gather all your courage and marshal your time effectively in the examination room.

Test-teaching companies hire professional test takers...people with good memories...who remember specific questions on tests and report them to the companies. The companies then use these to formulate their test books. Of course this means the civil service exams must constantly be revised. No matter. The test book you study will tend to be surprisingly close to what you will find on the examination.

If your community has a Business and Government Library, count yourself especially fortunate. Take advantage of this enormous resource for locating employers and likely job opportunities. Use the services of the reference librarian there, too. Information retrieval is his/her domain.

In my position as employment counselor for the California Employment Development Department, I conducted job search workshops for those in the professional, managerial, and technical fields. At these workshops I repeatedly stressed the value of using the Business and Government Library. I also insisted job hunters follow through promptly on every viable job opportunity. "Make the information pay off", was the theme. And it often did.

For example, one participant, Bob, reported at his last visit to the workshop, "While I was doing some research at the Business and Government Library, I overheard the librarian and a man near me discussing a particular job opening he had found. While he hesitated and delayed, I went to a telephone and called the company. The personnel manager asked me to come in that afternoon…" Bob paused, grinning.

"And…?" I probed.

Bob laughed. "And…I got the job."

PLAN NO. 9

NEW WAYS TO WORK

This is a changing world. Whether you see thorns or roses, obstacles or opportunities, depends upon your point of view. In the midst of change, opportunities take new forms. The process of changing anything–whether your clothes, your vacation, or your job, requires first changing your mind. This means with change you are in a position to improve the quality of life for yourself.

During a period of economic hard times, business cuts staff in an effort to reduce labor and management costs. One way to make the reduction is to establish varied hours and hire employees who are well trained and who can perform with little supervision.

This is happening right now in the current labor market. New staffing methods are making a definite impact on the way to locate a job. To take advantage of this, begin by changing how you look at conditions around you. Give a different position, a different course, and a different direction to your job search. Be flexible.

```
┌─────────────────────────────────────┐
│                                     │
│         *Strategy No. 25*           │
│                                     │
│    *REARRANGE YOUR WORK HOURS*      │
│                                     │
└─────────────────────────────────────┘
```

Are you are looking for a job? Then consider this. If you believe the only acceptable way to be employed is the traditional Monday to Friday, 8:00 to 5:00, start now rethinking that time worn pattern. Traditions may be convenient, but, over time, traditions have a way of becoming unwritten law. The 8:00 to 5:00 custom is not a law.

Flexibility inevitably undermines the accepted rules about the way the world should work. It's time to give up the notion that there is only one proper way and one proper time to be employed. New opportunities lie in expanding your options. You may well find the job you are looking for among some innovative ways to work

Flexibility always leads to interesting new possibilities. Here are some recent ones:

FLEX TIME

As the name indicates, this term originally applied to a full-time work week during which regular hours could be adjusted to the needs of individual employees. As long as the employee put in the required forty hours, it mattered little whether those hours were on a regular 8:00-5:00 schedule, 7:00-4:00, or 10:00-7:00.

Although specific "flex time" must by its nature be confined to jobs that have a clearly defined set of responsibilities, the concept of flexible time opened the door to other forms of flexible working. It now applies not only to unconventional hours, but to job sharing, leaves of absence, adaptable schedules, and even three 10-hour days per week.

JOB SHARING

Although this is an offshoot of "flex time", it is not as readily accepted by employers because there are at least two employees involved. Not only is the work divided, but some plan must be devised to divide the salary and benefits such as vacations, health care, and pensions between two employees.

Basically, "job sharing" works like this: First, the job duties must be of such a nature that tasks can be picked up readily by another or that they can be divided into clearly defined responsibilities. Tasks as structured as bookkeeping, accounts payable, customer service, individual client accounts, or work of a clearly technical nature are usually adjustable to the "job sharing" concept.

A job involving specific caseloads may also be divided between job sharing employees when the cases are assigned as distinctly different projects.

For example: One counselor for a community college might wish to share her position with another counselor, allowing each to balance career and family. The first counselor handles her student referrals Monday through midday Wednesday. The second woman takes the job with her assigned counselees for the rest of the week. The two employees divide one job evenly for both salary and benefits.

Since this job sharing method involves a number of changes in the administrative reporting, anyone wishing to request this plan must be prepared to sell the idea to the employer. The employer will want to know how the method works, how long the employees expect the sharing to last, and what happens if one of them leaves. In short, the job sharers must allay the employer's fears about the effect this will have on production.

MOTHER HOURS

Many mothers of young children must contribute to the family income. Some companies are willing to offer "mother hours." These hours might run from 8:30 a.m. to 2 p.m., or 9 a.m. to 3 p.m., depending on the employer's needs or the children's school schedules.

Custom tailoring the work schedules allows women to be home with children after school and during the summer. Frequently working mothers find that jobs at small retail stores and the fast food chains provide needed flexibility. Banks, savings and loans, hospitals, sometimes schools and colleges, and some technical jobs offer part-time positions which may lend opportunities for "mother-hours" scheduling. Job possibilities are not limited, however.

V-TIME

This designation refers to work time voluntarily reduced by agreement between the employee and the employer. Employees may reduce work time anywhere from 2% to 20% (occasionally up to 50%).

MOONLIGHTING

Some industrious workers take on more than one job in their struggle to make ends meet. This process, working a second job, sometimes more, after a full eight hours on one, is customarily described as "moonlighting". "Moonlighters" often work extra hours on weeknights and more on Saturdays.

Here are some actual examples:

1. One chemist works days in his profession, and eight hours pulling plywood on the "swing" shift in a sawmill.

2. A nurse works days. After regular hours she puts in four hours every weeknight and still more hours Saturdays as a telephone marketer.

3. An aspiring stand-up comedian works as a city tour guide during week days and as an entertainer in night clubs during evenings.

4. A full time postal clerk starts an early eight-hour

day at the post office and continues to work in the late afternoon at a wholesale plant nursery during the gardening season.

5. A police officer and fingerprint analyst moonlights as a construction worker.

6. An interviewer works days for the state employment service and teaches adult classes in résumé making at a community college evenings.

7. A bookkeeper works days at a fund raising organization, then designs and constructs costumes for musical theater groups nights and weekends.

8. A female police officer spends her off hours modeling bridal gowns and also works as a security officer.

The experience and the contacts gained through "moonlighting" may well open the door to getting a permanent, more desirable job with a new employer.

PART -TIME

The part time worker is usually employed less than 32 hours per week. The job often is permanently part-time.

TEMPORARY

The temporary worker may be employed full time for a limited period. This type of work is usually found in areas such as accounting, health care, engineering, and in seasonal work.

SHIFT WORK

Any industry or service that is maintained twenty-four hours a day divides the day into three eight-hour shifts. The first shift of the day is called "the day shift." The second shift, into the evening, is the "swing shift," and the night shift is the "graveyard shift." Starting hours of the shifts vary according to specific industry requirements.

Usually the swing shift and especially the graveyard shift are considered the less desirable work assignments, consequently the possibilities for job openings are greater then.

Strategy No. 26

RECONSIDER YOUR WORK PLACE

Telecommuting is an innovative new way to work involving the use of electronics and telecommunications devices. Instead of making long, difficult commutes to work each day, fighting stress, and contributing to heavy pollution on the nation's highways, more and more workers use modems, second phone lines, Call Waiting, voice mail, high speed digital and data capabilities, fax machines, and personal computers to carry out their job duties at home.

Workers reason that if job duties keep an individual before a computer all day, what difference does it make where the computer is located? Gradually, corporate employers are coming to accept the concept of telecommuting.

TELECOMMUTING

Among the many new expressions entering our vocabulary, is the term "Virtual Valley." To move to Virtual Valley implies a decision to leave the hectic pace of Silicon Valley (or its counterpart) and to join the growing number of telecommuters who have found ways to be productive via telephone and computer.

So rapid is the trend toward telecommuting that analysts find it hard to arrive at a solid figure. One estimate suggests the number of 7 million people nationwide working with computers at home. Another analyst says 9.1 million.

Charles Grantham, president of the Oakland (California) based Institute for the Study of Distributed Work reports that about 15% of the nation's white-collared workers will be telecommuting by the year 2000. Obviously, the speed of expansion will rapidly accelerate since the current rate is about 2%.

While telecommuting is not yet generally accepted by the majority of businesses, the level of involvement has doubled during the last five years.

When the San Francisco-Oakland Bay Bridge was severely damaged during the October, 1989, earthquake, several large corporations allowed employees to work at home while the bridge was being repaired. This introduced employers to other possibilities for telecommuting.

Employers who have been willing to experiment with telecommuting for their employees report increased productivity and less absenteeism. Employees feel less stress, less fatigue, are more inclined to be enthusiastic about their work and more loyal to the company.

Rather than work-at-home arrangements some companies sponsor satellite work centers at a distance from the main office. These satellite centers are generally located in communities where many of their employees live.

Pacific Bell Telephone has experimented with telecommuting for several years. This company has become a leader in setting up satellite offices so employees can avoid long commutes and traffic congestion.

Among the corporate employers who now accept the idea of telecommuting are: Levi Strauss and Company ; Charles Schwab Corporation, the national brokerage firm; Bancroft Whitney, a legal textbook publisher; Pacific Gas and Electric; and high tech firms such as Apple Computer and Hewlett Packard. Aetna, American Express, J.C. Penney Co., and Travelers Insurance are also exploring the use of telecommuting. The list grows.

So far telecommuting has been introduced in the large urban areas, but its possibilities for those workers who live in rural areas are apparent.

Rural Voice, a joint publication of Oregon's Independent Telephone Companies, offers a strong note of encouragement to their rural customers, declaring, "Telecommuting's time has come. By utilizing the digital switching technology which small telephone companies make available to their subscribers, many rural commuters could become telecommuters."

According to a study done for the Small Business Administration, a telecommuter can set up a home business with a computer, a telephone, and a fax machine for about $5000.00.

SUMMARY

As more businesses are structured to perform within the limitations of a core staff, employers need to retain employees who have multiple skills, who adjust readily to new assignments, and who can operate with a minimum of supervision. To keep these employees, employers are more likely to allow flex time, flex schedules, telecommuting, and other innovative work plans.

After lengthy work experience on an 8 to 5 schedule, you may find new work hours awkward at first. Once you have adjusted to them, however, you will discover more day hours in which to pursue a fuller personal life.

New ways to work can open up opportunities for further education in the field of your choice, or advanced training in your specialty. You can devote more time to family. On or off a job, it can be an emancipating experience.

PLAN NO. 10

DEVELOP AN INCOME PORTFOLIO

Extreme conditions call for extreme measures. If you've tried all the strategies for finding jobs up to this point, and you are still unemployed, here's that extreme measure: Have you ever thought of being a 'jack-of-all-trades'?

"Ridiculous," you say, "Everybody knows 'the jack-of-all-trades' is master of none".

Wrong. Jack may not be a specialist, but he collects and uses every skill he can muster. Now there's a practical man.

"Master of none?" On the contrary. The jack of all trades is a master of survival. When have you ever been able to summon a skilled handyman on the spot? The skilled handyman, otherwise known as "jack-of-all-trades," is a man in demand.

To be realistic, I do not suggest that you go out on the road to unplug sinks, replace window screens, or repair leaky faucets. (Not unless these are your skills, that is.) What I suggest is that the jack-of-all-trades has a successful way of earning a living. Your own special talents may well fit into such a mode of operation.

The jack-of-all-trades has a work style worth considering. This applies to the 'jill-of-all-trades', too.

1. He or she knows exactly what his/her talents are.

2. He applies them in different combinations to meet the demands of different jobs.

3. He has an unfailing contingency plan. Multiple jobs mean multiple sources of income. He combines a number of employers. This eliminates the possibility that he will be completely laid off.

4. By diversifying, he reduces risk from factors peculiar to one particular company, risk such as seasonal activity, loss of funding, or union strikes.

5. His income may be irregular, but that's not likely with a skilled handyman. (During a major emergency, you will find that customers have booked his services days ahead.)

6. Through customers and suppliers, he taps into the hidden jobs for his talents. He can usually count on satisfied customers to refer him to friends or neighbors. Suppliers frequently offer suggestions leading to other jobs. For him, advertising is not a budget breaker.

7. He keeps his skills and his tools up to date. That's good management. (We're still thinking in terms of either he or she, remember.)

8. He sets up his own schedule, although it may mean a hybrid composite of flex time, part time, temporary, job sharing, on call, or other. In short, he is flexible.

9. Jack supplies his own benefits. He pays his own self-employment tax (15.3% of income).

10. He is a successful independent contractor, his own boss.

In this amazing world, the jack-of-all-trades, reputedly "master of none", has become the role model for an army of jobless midmanagers and other professionals. Unemployment makes strange bedfellows. It also opens a lot of eyes to new possibilities.

An increasing number of workers, cast adrift, have begun to reassess their futures. Many people are finding that they don't want to be limited to one job forty hours a week. Partly angered at being dumped unceremoniously, partly exhilarated by their new freedom, they are rebelling. No longer will they accept the notion that they are dependent on the whims of management for their survival.

Unemployment is a universal leveler. Whether you are among the high and mighty or the lowly and humble you still stand in the same line at the employment office.

It can be an ego-shattering experience.

On the other hand, unemployment can mean a great opportunity to rebuild your working life. This is the time to issue your own declaration of independence. Rebel. Ideas plus courage and persistence can get you out of that long line at the employment office.

Many bright, rebellious people have decided to put all of their talents to use. They have begun to identify themselves as a bundle of assets to be invested in new ways.

You know about stock portfolios which involve the business of making decisions about when and where you will invest your discretionary money. Today we are seeing the emergence of a new option: the INCOME PORT-FOLIO. This is the business of making the decisions about when and where you will invest your time and talents.

You may be aware, too, that your former jobs failed to tap your many talents. Are you fed up with being limited to a few skills you have that someone else finds useful? Or are you beginning to realize that you, too, have a bundle of unused talents. Are you going to let these go stale and shrivel up, or are you going to invest them to bring in the income you need?

How about setting up your own income portfolio? Your talents and resources are the assets you will invest. Place value on every skill, every experience, every success. Then look for ways to use each one. When you have made a comprehensive inventory of these, you are ready to invest in yourself.

The jack-of-all-trades is actually the pioneer of the new trend. Accustomed to using a number of skills, he has long ago identified a fallback position if the need for one arises. His handyman activities make up a hybrid composite, the work style in the income portfolio.

This may sound very radical. Actually it's an ancient process. Parents and teachers warned you and me about such a course of action. Unfortunately, the old bromide about the jack-of-all-trades forced us to lower our sights. We were told to pick a career, any career, so long as it offered prestige and money, and prepare for a working life with a single focus. Variety and flexibility were not acceptable choices. Now, in a time of severe unemployment, variety and flexibility are the only acceptable choices.

Workers, giving up the notion that they are dependent on one organization and one line of work for their survival, are striking out in new directions.

How does business respond to the new trends in worker independence? Having reduced their working force to core staffs, business and industry are finding that they need a staff with multiple talents and flexibility. In short, the new worker.

Business and industry, in the effort to reduce labor costs and still keep key workers, are offering their own hybrid composites. In addition to the pay check, they may add other inducements to keep their most vital workers: Child care, paid parental leave, or portable pension plans.

Flexible schedules allow workers to pursue a second vocation, a community project, or a hobby. The whole work field is changing.

Probably, if you are going to be one of the new workers, you will not identify yourself as a jack-of-all-trades at your next class reunion. You will hold your head high and announce confidently that you are "developing an income portfolio." Same thing.

So, how are you going to develop this "income portfolio."

How do you get started?

The steps in making an investment of any kind are the same:

1. List your assets. Specifically, what have you done in your life that others find useful or enjoyable or encouraging or helpful or accurate or dependable or beautiful or delightful or protective or informative or comforting or healthful or necessary? (You started such a list in Plan No. 2.) Each of these activities is job producing.

2. List every proof of your accumulated experience. This means tasks you have performed, problems you have solved. All these are part of your marketable abilities.

3. If you are already employed but expect the ax to fall any day, start now putting together a contingency plan. This might mean a plan to start a sideline business, or

collect information on varied full-time or part-time jobs plus self-employment.

4. Knowing that some businesses offer special inducements in lieu of higher salaries, think about what privileges you will accept as part pay. To attract skilled workers on a contingency basis, some employers are offering child care, parental leave, and freedom to pursue a second job or a hobby.

5. Consider what your own hybrid composite might include: Flex time; job sharing; multiple jobs; home office; on call substituting; or commercializing your hobbies. It certainly will involve courage, self-confidence, and drive. An income portfolio is not for the faint hearted.

6. What barter opportunities can you discover? Whatever you barter for increases your discretionary income by reducing cost.

7. Remember: One man's need is another man's opening. Opportunity for interesting work is everywhere, but it takes a creative or inventive mind to discover it.

Based on your talents and resources, the INCOME PORTFOLIO is the tangible result of personal effort, creativity, inventiveness, flexibility, and willingness to adjust to new situations.

Let's look at some examples:

INCOME PORTFOLIO #1

I first met Sue when she came to me for help in getting a job. Sue, 18, was a recent high school graduate. She hoped to enter college in the fall. Money from the family was out of the question. Family resources were severely drained by the needs of several younger brothers and sisters.

As an employment counselor with the Youth Opportunity Center, I was inundated with scores of eager young teenagers also looking for employment of some kind. Jobs for recent graduates were scarce. Nevertheless Sue refused to be discouraged. She was determined she would earn enough during the summer to cover her first expenses in September. Then she fully expected to keep on finding work as the months went on.

I gave her some suggestions, promised to look for something suitable, and sent Sue on her way. Two days later she called. "Never mind, Mrs. Cooper, I have enough work," she reported, "I have four jobs that cover seven days a week. I can't handle any more."

Before the concept of an income portfolio was named, Sue had begun to develop her own. She had taken inventory of her skills, most of which had been in volunteer activities, and offered these skills to friends and neighbors. She had also pursued part-time and temporary jobs she found in the classified ads.

She knew she was skilled in caring for children. After all, she had had plenty of experience at home. She was used to house cleaning. There was plenty of that at home, too. She had been successful selling cookies door to door to raise money for her class activities. And she knew how to cook.

From these varied experiences and skills Sue now had put together seven days of full time work every week. True, the days were with several employers: Child care for working mothers, house-cleaning with two, cooking for elderly retirees and helping with the daily chores. The rest of the week she was busy in a fast food restaurant. Sue had become a jack-of-all- trades, and a master of her unemployment.

Having learned to use every talent and skill, plus courage and determination, Sue had taken her first steps to financial independence. Sue would always find ways to be employed.

INCOME PORTFOLIO #2

Today independent nurses are making a comeback. They make house calls, give physical exams, and routine tests, and make recommendations for further care. On occasion they provide long term care. Commonly the independent nurse tends to childbirths and women's health care.

This is variety and versatility in action. Here the investment is a finely honed skill, offered to a series of patients in their own homes. The variety lies in the combination of skills in different forms, plus the variety of families into which the nurse goes. Versatility is necessary in order to function successfully under frequently changing work environments.

INCOME PORTFOLIO #3

B.W. teaches people how to be jobless without being discouraged. She has been the owner of an industrial products company and a mail order business. She has also done marketing and consulting work. "Stepping out on your own involves developing multiple sources of income," she says.

Taking her own advice, she conducts seminars, publishes a monthly newsletter for small business hopefuls, and does free lance writing. Added to these, she has begun a catering business. On the side she also teaches adult education.

INCOME PORTFOLIO #4

S.R., a new business management teacher at the secondary level, was caught between the flood of new teachers and a severe cutback in school funding. Unable to locate a full time teaching position, he put his income portfolio together by combining various talents.

S.R. now worked as a very successful on-call substitute teacher for two high schools during school hours. After school and on weekends, he coached basketball and football. On the side he painted a friend's house.

For a time he also worked a fourth job as a ware-houseman in a janitorial supply company until he ran out of hours in each twenty four. When he didn't have enough hours left to offer the janitorial supply company, he quit that work.

Strategy No. 27

BE A FREE AGENT. DEVELOP YOUR OWN INCOME PORTFOLIO

Audrey Freedman, executive director of the Conference Board, a privately financed research organization in New York, predicts a "contingent" labor force of free-lancers and consultants will provide services to businesses, industry, and households. She says, "The next fourteen years, the present instability will create millions of jobs that have not been formally categoried."

The jack-of-all-trades and his INCOME PORT-FOLIO work style is the forerunner.

PLAN NO. 11

YOU CALL THE TUNE

Some of the things we might wish never happened may become the channels for new successes. Unemployment certainly is one of those things.

If you are looking for a job guarantee, develop your own successful small business. Small businesses naturally create a wealth of hidden jobs and offer the potential for security and advancement.

Does a small business seem unduly risky? It is if your small business is built on a fantasy. It should evolve from a discovery you have made, from the development of an idea, from the answer to a community need, or from a well-practiced hobby. You will need a definite goal, strong drive, detailed planning, persistence, and knowledge of effective business practices to be a successful owner.

Your first experience with a business of your own may have been the lemonade stand in the front yard. Nowadays the lemonade may be Kool Aid, but the appeal is still the same: carrying out your own project, and enjoying the heady feeling of being an entrepreneur. And who would hazard a guess as to how many successful small businesses in adulthood ultimately evolved from the joy of that small beginning as a child?

The pioneer of a new business, whether it be one that offers ideas, information, services, or products, is the entrepreneur of the future. If you have a do-it-yourself philosophy and a commitment to self respect and self reliance, you probably tend to be innovative, a necessity in a business of your own.

Not everybody has the urge to create a small business of his own. The small businessman (or woman) in the beginning is a kind of one-man band.

As you may know, the usual one-man band has a harmonica in his mouth, a banjo on his lap, cymbals between his knees, horns and bells tied to his sides, and a bass drum at his feet. By vigorous effort and much flailing about he produces a frenetic performance, passes the hat, and hopes confidently for a better day tomorrow.

The early months, even years, of a small business operation require the owner/creator to play a number of "instruments." As "INVENTOR," he devises the product or service that will be the backbone of the business, and sets about to develop it. He is the "ASSEMBLER" in manufacturing the product and sets out as "SALES MANAGER" to market it. He acts as "PURCHASING AGENT" for whatever materials and equipment are needed to produce his product and furnish the office. As

"ADVERTISING MANAGER," he determines the advertising and promotion. As "SHIPPING CLERK" he handles the inventory, and does the packaging.

Back in the office, he is the "GENERAL MANAGER" who raises the money needed to finance the business operations and deals with the lenders. Along the line he is a combination "SECRETARY" and "BOOKKEEPER." At the end of a very long day, he becomes the "JANITOR," grabs a broom and sweeps out. All this takes motivation, determination, persistence, and courage. These, too, are the qualities of a pioneer.

In a sweat shirt and jeans, driving a ten-year-old pickup the entrepreneur (one who creates a small business) may not fit the standard picture of "a knight in shining armor." Yet, he it is, who is the mover in the economic recovery, the hope of the nation.

Good times will follow job pioneers. Does it happen? Yes. Even if you, the small business man or woman are only moderately successful, you have at the very least, made a job for yourself. If your ideas prove to be more successful, you begin to hire others to help you. Now you have reduced the unemployment lines, not only by putting yourself to work, but by the amount of employment you have created for others.

As time goes by, you may eventually expand the current activities or devise more new businesses, solve perplexing problems, create new jobs, and put scores of people back to work.

Logically, the entrepreneurs will be the movers in the recovery. How does this happen? Let's look at the statistics: The Small Business Administration, in the "State of Small Business" as reported to the President in the fall of 1991 states:

"The IRS received 20.4 million non-farm tax returns for 1990. These included both large and small businesses. Of these 1990 returns, there were: 4.4 million corporations; 1.8 million partnerships; 14.2 million sole proprietorships, for a total of 20.4 million businesses."

"Out of that vast total, [20.4 million businesses], approximately 7000 are large businesses, i.e. 500 or more employees."

Usually job seekers, looking for employment, head straight for the 7000, but the majority of jobs are not found there. With simple arithmetic, (20,400,000 million minus 7000) we find that there are 20,393,000 small businesses employing from one to five hundred employees each in 1990. There are even more of these small businesses emerging at the present time.

If each of the small businesses hired only the owner and one other person, that would amount to 40,786,000 jobs. However the broad definition of small business employment (1 to 500) implies many, many more jobs. Obviously, small business is the backbone of our economy.

With a changing estimate of 6.8 million people out of work, as of Spring, 1994, the creation of more new businesses is imperative. He who devises new methods, invents new products, and supplies useful ideas will not only advance himself, but he will promote the prosperity of the nation.

Creating a unique small business requires strong motivation, the willingness to learn, and a burning desire to carry the project to completion. If this describes you, then you have the characteristics leading to success in a business of your own.

Many people are interested. They will say, "I want a small business of my own," but they fail to finish the sentence. " A small business doing…" what? Few have thought beyond a vague desire.

I saw this vividly demonstrated when I sat in on a new community college class entitled, "Starting a Small Business of Your Own." From the first evening, the instructor insisted the class begin drawing up formal business plans. This assignment at the right time would have been correct, but only about three students out of a class of more than twenty had made any decision about what kind of business they hoped to develop. Lacking a focus, the students' attendance dropped off rapidly.

There are many classes on small business available, books and more books devoted to the processes of establishing a business, a plethora of information at hand in and out of government agencies, free and inexpensive help from the Small Business Administration, and unlimited self- help advice, but where can you get guidance in making the choice of a specific business? Small businesses grow from definite ideas.

You will never get started until you have decided what your business will be. Begin with an inventory of your interests, your unpressured choice of activities. If you must be married to your new business, (as is inevitable to get started), it should be activities you would spend time on, paid for or not.

Here's an example of the kind of dedication that carries on through thick and thin and is a good predictor of success in a new business:

Brian Steffen has a premier motorcycle repair shop, QUALITY MOTOR CYCLE REPAIR in Mill Valley, California. Why did he pick this business? He says, "All my life I've had a compulsion to take things apart, to see what makes them tick, to figure out how to make them better, then put them back together. I've been doing it since I was a kid. Now look what I'm doing. I'm getting paid for my compulsion. How much better life is there?"

To decide what form your business might take, first search current newspapers and other such publications to see what others have done. You will find the new businesses fall into several distinct categories.

1. Information clearinghouses

2. Solutions to needs of special individuals

3. Solutions to community needs

4. Hobbies turned into commercial ventures because they appeal to a definite market

5. Inventions

6. Services not yet supplied, or inadequately supplied elsewhere

7. A special niche not otherwise covered

8. A unique skill

9. Different approaches to services or products already on the market

Nowhere else will you locate such a rich source of information on individual small businesses than in the pages of your daily newspapers. Here you will find a constant stream of reports on small businesses built on the ideas of the average citizen. Sometimes, you can even pick up valuable tips on running a small business from the owners' comments quoted in the news.

Let's explore some of the possibilities by categories.

Strategy #28

SET UP A CLEARING HOUSE

People are hungry for information. Information centers are proliferating, and for good reason. Not long ago,

147

we were told knowledge doubles in five years. Today it is estimated knowledge doubles every ninety days.

Information centers have various focuses. Here are several needs reported by newspapers. Also some innovative solutions:

HOW DO I GET INTO PUBLIC RECORDS FOR INFORMATION?

Using computers and telephone lines to search through reams of public records, Frank Dillon, managing director of MPC Telcom and Charles Pinck, private investigator, bring their investigative skills to their recently established DETECTIVE INFORMATION NETWORK in Annandale, Virginia.

Dillon and Pinck check out promoters who offer "the investment of a lifetime," locate missing heirs, track deadbeats, and even find old loves.

Using the computer, they can do a simple search or analyze what your (the caller's) problem is, and offer information to solve the problem. If the answer lies in simple data, the two investigators show you how to get the information you require, supplying sources, the addresses and even telephone numbers.

WHERE DO I FIND A COMPETENT AUTO MECHANIC?

Dana Deselle and Megan Carmichael recognized the consumers' need for information on competent automobile mechanics. They also found repair shops wanted more customers. By combining the two needs, the women created a new business. (800) FIX A CAR now provides car repair referrals to anyone between Fresno and San Diego

HOW DOES ONE LOCATE
RELIABLE TRADES PEOPLE?

Nancy Roberts founded SACRAMENTO TRADES GUILD, a service that helps consumers locate reliable, licensed trades people. Home maintenance is often a problem. From the leaking roof, leaking faucet, to shifting foundation, whatever the repairs needed, all consumers hope to find a reliable contractor to do the work. The Trades Guild supplies information on screened and approved contractors.

HOW CAN THE SKILLS OF
MBA STUDENTS BE USED?

PROPHET MARKET RESEARCH is the joint effort of Scott Galloway and Ian Chaplin, 1992 MBA graduates from University of California, Berkeley. Their consulting business is a network of first year MBA students from top business schools in the nation.

"They'll act as our field reps, collecting data for our corporate clients from their respective regions. They'll also be available to market a client's product to the campus community," Galloway explains.

HOW CAN A SOLO TRAVELER
MAKE FRIENDLY CONTACTS?

If you are single and travel alone, Jane Doefer, Cambridge, Massachusetts, writer, has your interests at heart. Feeling that resorts and restaurants did not serve the interests of the solo traveler adequately, Ms. Doefer started a newsletter called "GOING SOLO" to provide information on meeting others and having a good time while going it alone.

I NEED A SPECIAL BOOK.
CAN YOU HELP ME FIND IT?

Genevieve Krueger is a book detective. She works out of her rustic home nestled in the foothills of Los Angeles. Finding rare or hard-to-find books that others want, she says, is eminently satisfying. In her crusade she is part of a small network of people who perform searches for individuals. Many of her successes fulfill memories for her clients and their joy is one of the rewards in the book sleuthing business.

I WORK AND NEED HELP
CHECKING ON MY CHILDREN AND
ELDERLY PARENTS.
WHERE CAN I GET IT?

In Concord, California, Jan Eversole's company, CALL CARE, is a computerized calling service that checks to see that latch key children and elderly people are where they are supposed to be and are all right.

HOW CAN I LOCATE A
RELIABLE NURSING HOME?

In a similar pattern, for a fee a licensed nursing home specialist, Jane Perlow, of Great Neck, New York, offers her services to families who need help locating a suitable nursing home for loved ones in New York State.

A Florida company, HEALTHCARE INFONET, has taken this idea into the computer age, marketing a database nationwide that provides names, addresses, phone and the individuals to be contacted, for 10,000 home health care providers.

ONE MAN'S TRASH CAN BE ANOTHER MAN'S
TREASURE. IS THERE A WAY TO LOCATE
USABLE INDUSTRIAL WASTE?

PACIFIC MATERIALS EXCHANGE of Spokane, Washington, has developed a computer network for the 23 waste exchanges in North America.

Directories published by various industrial exchange services provide a system of intermediaries for the selling and buying of industrial waste. Pacific Materials Exchange recently listed 400 waste items available in the Northwest.

In Syracuse, N.Y. the NORTHEAST INDUSTRIAL EXCHANGE serves a similar purpose.

HOW DO I LOCATE A
POTENTIAL BUYER FOR MY BUSINESS?

BUSINESS PARTNERSHIPS, INC., at Woodland Hills in Los Angeles County, locates prospective small business buyers or partners and matches them up with small business sellers.

Business Partnerships promotes a gradual, orderly transition helping buyer and seller to work together.

Strategy #29

RIDE YOUR HOBBY TO WORK

Build your business around your hobby, but beware of judging the market from your own enthusiasm. Your choice of hobby is not necessarily what someone else wants. Your hobby must benefit others if you expect those people to pay you to pursue it.

HIS HARMONICA BECAME
HIS BUSINESS

Jon Gindick likes harmonicas. Well, that's not quite right. Actually Jon is passionate about his music and the harmonica allows him to share his love with others.

The harmonica appeals to all kinds of people because it is affordable, fairly easy to play, and is certainly portable. On that basis Jon Gindick wrote and self-published his first how to book on playing the harmonica. Now his current book *"COUNTRY AND BLUES HARMONICA FOR THE MUSICALLY HOPELESS"* packed in a red net bag with the harmonica, sells very well. The book and harmonica kit moves 100,000 copies annually.

Jon advises others who want to make a business of what they love to do. "Start small," he says. "Make a cassette tape to teach others how to do what you do best. Allow your product to create a market for you."

THE FUNNY SIDE OF FAMILY LIFE

Cartoonist Gail Machlis, one of just ten nationally syndicated female columnists in the country, explores kids, careers, and relationships. She creates her cartoons from bits of family life in Berkeley, California.

GARDENING HOBBY BECOMES PROFITABLE

Former San Ramon High School history teacher Stefanie Delmont has converted her sprawling backyard in Orinda, California, to a vegetable garden that produces enough produce to fill a pickup truck each week. On Saturdays, she joins other green grocers to sell her harvest at the Pleasant Hill farmers market.

MANAGEMENT RESPONDS TO MAGIC

Lisa Menna took up magic as a hobby to help defray her college expenses. As time went by, she combined her performing skills with her knowledge of psychology, marketing, and entrepreneurship. She now performs corporate magic shows to illustrate major marketing and strategy points at company presentations.

A CLASSIC COLLECTION

Beth Shimkin in El Segundo, California, is president of a company that buys and refurbishes classic telephones. RING MY BELL, her company, depends on word of mouth to spread news to collectors and sellers of the phones. Being close to television and movie studios, the company is frequently called up to supply phones for props.

HE BUILDS MUSEUM QUALITY MINIATURE RACING CARS

What kind of work do race car drivers graduate to? At one time after he quit racing, Don Edmunds built customized cars for elite drivers. Now out of Carpenterville, Oregon, Edmunds builds highly crafted miniatures of those racing cars for collectors.

DEDICATED FAN TURNS HOBBY INTO BUSINESS.

Bobby Plapinger likes baseball and anything remotely connected to it. He collects books on baseball, fiction and nonfiction, selling from his private collection. He has biographies, anthologies, mysteries, autobiographies, even astrological charts, all stacked floor to ceiling of a room in his home at Ashland, Oregon. The excess overflows into the hall outside. Twice a year, in time for

Opening Day and the World Series, he publishes a catalog listing the titles for sale.

SHE CARVES CHRISTMAS TRADITIONS

Susan Hoekstra found a wooden Santa that she liked in a Portland specialty shop. Fortunately, she couldn't afford the $300 price tag. This led her to take a carving class at Linn-Benton Community College.

She proved to be an especially adept student, turning out whimsical Santas that were picked up in limited editions by LE FEVERS SANTA'S COMPANY in Molalla, Oregon. In her Corvallis home, Susan creates her fantasy Santas part of the year, and makes and sells beautiful quilts the rest of the time.

OLD FASHIONED FLOWERS BLOSSOM INTO NATIONWIDE BUSINESS

Lisbeth Farmar Bowers missed the old fashioned flowers she knew as a girl. Since they weren't available in florist shops, she decided to grow her own. The result is SONOMA FLOWER COMPANY in California.

The company began as a roadside stand. Those flowers that didn't sell were worked into dried arrangements which sold to mail order companies. From this she and her daughters hit farmers' markets. Professional designers began asking for her flowers, and she found herself in the shipping business. Ultimately her flowers appeared on royal visits and presidential inaugurations.

```
┌─────────────────────────────────────┐
│                                     │
│           Strategy No. 30           │
│                                     │
│        SHARE YOUR INVENTION         │
│                                     │
│                                     │
└─────────────────────────────────────┘
```

The world moved forward when the wheel was invented. Your invention may not be that important, but it could be marketable.

POUCH FOILS PICKPOCKETS

Howard Geschwind of Bonita, California has patented a pouch which encloses the wallet and is closed with Velcro. It sticks when pickpockets try to remove it.

MOP DOLL KITS

Pat Leslie decided it would be convenient to have a complete kit at hand for young guests to put mop dolls together when they come for a visit. The kits include all materials and accessories, come in different colors, and can be assembled in about three hours.

STROLLER BUILT FOR JOGGING

In Yakima, Washington, RACING STROLLERS, INC., owned by Phil Baechler and his wife, Mary, is the outcome of Phil's inventive talents. The Baechlers added a Super Jogger and a Walk-A-Bout to the Racing Stroller. These allow the babies to go along for the ride when their parents are jogging.

LESSON ON PLASTICS SPAWNS
MULTI-MILLION DOLLAR BUSINESS

Tom Killion, high school teacher, was teaching students at Ben Davis High School in Indianapolis about plastics. From that class came an idea for a bendable pencil.

Two years later, after a lot of experimentation, Tom had a pencil that could be molded and would bend without breaking. The first year 500,000 BENTCILS (as he called them) sold through mail order catalogs.

By 1992, BENTAL COMPANY produced more than ten million units and a sales total of nearly five million dollars. Tom Killion's idea has expanded to employ 90 full and part-time workers.

PET SHAMPOOING NATURALLY

She didn't start out to capitalize on the growing interest in "natural-type pet products". Actually Stalle Pavlides was hoping to find a camouflage for vitiligo. What she wound up with was a nontoxic, chemical-free herbal dog and cat shampoo.

Now her business, NATURALLY YOURS, ALEX (the company is named after Alex, her Airedale) is showing a brisk growth in sales and promise for the future.

IT PAYS TO FLY A KITE

A few years back, Jim (Red) McClarran and a friend bought a kite to fly along the coast on a beach vacation. The kite wouldn't fly. McClarran took this as a challenge. He swore he would invent kites guaranteed to fly.

The result is his booming business, JET KITES, based on methodical formulas to make adjustments for speed, control, range, and maneuverability. The Rockaway Beach, Oregon, factory with sales above one million dollars annually, employs women to sew kites in their homes, while other employees at the factory assemble the complete product for shipment overseas.

NEW METHOD PROVIDES CLASSICALLY ELEGANT COLUMNS

Frank Harris, of Castro Valley, California, cement mason and inventor, began designing fiber optic systems for swimming pools and driveways. From this he applied his computerized drawing program to designing concrete shaping forms made of inexpensive plastic foam.

The product, which he calls MAGIC COLUMN, is a new method for shaping self supporting concrete. The foam forms replace cardboard which is less sturdy, and fiberglass and steel tubing which are costly.

Custom designed columns shaped in Harris's forms

are appearing in a number of projects such as the Embassy Suites Hotel at Burlingame, California.

TINY ADS ON CASH REGISTER RECEIPTS

VAL-Q-PONS INTERNATIONAL has discovered a new advertising medium. The small San Ramon (California) company prints eye catching ads and coupons in full color on the back of cash register receipts. "We're doing things differently, and it's obviously paid off for us," says Hal Brin, co-founder.

ALERT ALARM FOR BOATS

Los Angeles inventor, Willis Boyden, concerned that people become overconfident in their recreational boating, has developed a boat warning device to signal "abandon ship" when the boat takes on a dangerous level of water.

HE INVENTS INGENIOUS DEVICES
FOR THE DISABLED

John Cains is a retired flight engineer, but he is far happier designing for the disabled. As he tells it, "I started going to boat shows, and I noticed how hard it was for people in wheelchairs to get around at a boat show." He decided to do something about it.

Beginning as a basement operation in his home, Cains's business, GRANDMAR, has now become an important supplier to equipment for the disabled.

GRANDMAR employes seven full time employees and two part time workers. The business now occupies an old warehouse with more than 10,000 square feet of space. Here Cains sells, rents, services, modifies, and repairs wheelchairs, and he also invents specialized aids for the disabled.

Helping the disabled, he says, "is a lot more satisfying and fun than flying a Boeing 747 around the world." Smiles on the faces of the disabled are a special reward.

Strategy #31

FIND YOUR NICHE

You may already know what your skills are. Now be creative about where your customers are.

GUITAR-MAKERS ATTRACT CUSTOMERS BY SUPERIOR WORK

With a few weeks of painstaking work, John Mello, at his home in Kensington, California will fashion different woods and metal, a bit of ivory, bone, or plastic and a short length of suede, into a hand-crafted concert guitar.

Although he lives and works in the San Francisco Bay Area, his reputation for his workmanship extends far beyond. Named one of the country's top 20 classical guitar makers by Musician Magazine, John Mello attracts customers largely by word of mouth.

Greg Lowry of Walnut Creek, California, on the other hand, specializes in designing headless guitars. With the headless guitar, the tuning pegs are placed in the body of the instrument near the bridge. The tuning block inserted in that position enriches the resonance of the guitar.

Lowry constructs his custom made guitars with exotic materials such as rosewood and burled maple. When he first launched his business as a guitar inventor and maker, he supplemented his income with guitar repairs. To this he added his song writing skills leading to two top selling songs. Both exceeded one million sales.

When the guitar industry further pursues a campaign to educate youth in the value of music, Lowry expects to step up production. Meanwhile, top notch players learn about his masterpieces by word of mouth.

CLASSICAL WOODCARVING RETURNS TO FAVOR

Architecture banned ornamentation on structures for nearly a century. After years of stark forms and straight lines, the general public is rebelling. People are beginning to demand beauty and ornamentation.

This brings woodcarving back in style and woodcarvers into demand. Ian Agrell, a carver of monumental talent, is a classicist. His partner, Adam Thorpe, is the modernist. ANGRELL AND THORPE, LTD., with three other carvers and a gilder, work at Sausalito, California, where they form exquisite art for the elite.

161

"People are hearing of our work by word of mouth," Angrell says. Getting established has not been easy. There was a time each carver slept on the floor to save money. Now they take orders from clients such as the Sultan of Brunei, London's Kensington Palace, the Salt Lake City's Roman Catholic cathedral, the Victoria and Albert Museum, and other prosperous clients. In addition Agrell and Thorpe accept thirty students a year, at $3,000 for a 12 week course.

Thanks to the special skills and persistence of these men, woodcarving has moved again to its proper place as an art and a practical business.

HIS BUSINESS IS SELLING ROCKING CHAIRS

Matt Bearson has a talent for helping people relax...in rocking chairs. Rocking chairs are his specialty. His only specialty. Well, not really. Matt specializes in making people comfortable. The sale of the product is secondary and almost a certainty.

It all started when Matt began looking for a rocking chair for a friend. He found that rocking chairs were usually the ugly ducklings of the furniture flock, tucked away in the back somewhere and largely ignored.

He decided to do something about it. The result is 100 Percent Rocking Chair located in Los Angeles. These chairs may be of various constructions and designs, but the chairs all rock. By having a single specialty, Matt has another advantage, he doesn't have to deal with the intense competition found in the regular furniture market.

And then, most people like to rock. Matt makes it easy for them to do so. Refreshments in his store are encouraged. Every customer coming in is offered tea, coffee, spring water, or a soft drink, then invited to pick a chair, sit down and rock to soothing music. Relaxed and unrushed, customers buy.

Matt sells rocking chairs. The customers buy comfort.

FARM WAGON GREENGROCER

Rodolpho Lara found his place in the market. He takes his farm harvest directly to the ultimate consumer. Each day he picks fresh zucchini, onions, tomatoes, peppers, green beans, and corn from his fields near the BART (Bay Area Rapid Transit) station in Fremont, California. He sets up his own farmer's market in the back of his truck and sells to commuters as they return home from work.

HOT BREAD:
THE FRAGRANCE OF GRATITUDE

Each Christmas, Bill Hotchkiss, owner of SUNRISE SOURDOUGH BAKERY, Philomath, Oregon, has been baking 125 to 150 loaves of bread as a thank you gift to businesses and the community.

Bill opened the bakery in Philomath after learning his art at an organic bakery in Phillipston, Massachusetts.

His clients are natural foods outlets in Portland and Eugene, Oregon.

HE CREATES COFFEE BREAK TREATS

Law school had been Steve Sirianni's original goal, but after graduation from St. Mary's College, with some time to spare, he began experimenting with his grandmother's recipe for biscotti. He knew biscotti, an Italian treat described as a cross between a biscuit and a cookie, are especially favored by the coffee house crowd. Here was his ready made clientele.

When test marketing was successful, Sirianni found himself dedicated to the kitchen rather than the classroom. By now business was expanding so fast that he recruited two roommates, Tom Soldati and Richard Martin to handle the finance and marketing details.

NONNI'S BISCOTTI, named for Siriani's grandmother, has become the fastest growing biscotti manufacturer in the nation. Early sales of the Hayward (California) based business, surpassed $1 million.

Strategy #32

OFFER SERVICE

This could apply to services not yet available, or those inadequately supplied. Go beyond what your competitors do. Provide the extra help that brings the world to your door.

OLD FASHIONED SERVICE FUELS BUSINESS

In a dwindling market, Ken Betts has introduced a basic old fashioned strategy: good service, courtesy, and a smile. Betts owns eight service stations around the San Francisco Bay Area, including the East Bay.

Betts' secret is full automotive service: fill-ups, tows, complete interior and exterior car washes, tuneups, and major repair jobs. In this era of company operated stations, where the customer waits on himself, sticks his credit card in a slot, and never hears a personal hello or goodbye, Ken Betts' friendly service is a great magnet for customers.

BASICALLY SHE DRIVES...DIPLOMATICALLY

Several years ago, Kathi Kamen Goldmark's mother said, "There are people who drive authors around in their cars. It's something you should do." So Kathi became a media escort and found out her duties require much more than driving a car. Regularly, she is involved in escorting authors to personal appearances, book signings, and print, radio, or TV interviews. She now also trains her backup drivers, and through it all maintains enthusiasm and joie de vivre.

BODYGUARDS FOR BATTERED WOMEN

Gregory Kottke has a very busy bodyguard agency located in Milwaukee, but it hasn't turned out quite as he expected. He had planned to get his clients from politicians, movie stars, big business executives, and visiting professional athletes, or so he thought.

Instead Kottke, in cooperation with the Task Force on Battered Women has become a bodyguard for frightened women. The phone rings steadily, underscoring the demand for such protective services.

KIDS KABS RELIEVE
PARENTAL RUN AROUND

In Birmingham, Michigan, Pamela Henderson, a former high school physical education teacher and gymnastics coach, got fed up with the tough time working parents had getting their children to and from various after school activities.

One solution to the suburban runaround was to start a specialized transport service: KIDS KABS. Her company is her answer to several growing trends, such as the decline in adequate public transportation, the larger number of working mothers and single parents of both sexes, more extra-curricular activities for children, and the limited number of free hours in the day.

In operation, Kids Kab provides transportation at about half the cost of a taxi. Three full-time employees, seven part timers, ten vans and minivans, transport about 300 daily riders to their activities.

Strategy #33

SOLVE A COMMUNITY PROBLEM

The whole world needs help. Pick one perplexing difficulty. Find a way to correct it.

HE BUILT HIS FORTUNE
OUT OF THROW AWAY CANS

Working his way up from the ranks of the homeless, Chris Jeffers is prospering mightily. He has set up a business for redeeming aluminum cans at half their retail redemption price.

Jeffers rents an empty theater where people bring in what they have found the night before. Why do they sell him their cans at half price? Jeffers pays out immediate cash, an important consideration for street people.

Jeffers' small business is flourishing. He has acquired a truck and employs three full-time workers, and occasional casuals to help him accept and sort the cans.

LUXURY LIMOUSINE SERVICE
TO THE AIRPORT

Most flyers, frequent or not, are faced with the inevitable nuisance of getting from remote places to airports and from airports to other places equally as remote from airports. Whatever travel time is saved by flying is lost getting to and from the airport by public conveyances.

The schedules of individual shuttle vans do not always fit the customer's needs because the vans must make a number of stops. There is also a great need for transportation that can handle associations and large groups, especially those whose participants want to meet and then leave, not stay over for a weekend. Travel time to and from airports is wasted business time, so Bill Wheeler of Pleasanton, California, set about to solve these problems.

His new venture, Black Tie Airport Express, has launched a regularly scheduled direct bus service to San Francisco International (on the west side of the San Francisco Bay) from Concord, Walnut Creek, and Lafayette (inland on the east side).

The buses stop at two major hotels in Concord, two major hotels in Walnut Creek, and a major hotel in Lafayette. Then the buses go directly to S.F. International. Buses will roll on regular schedule every 60 to 90 minutes, seven days a week. These arrangements solve the twin problems of erratic scheduling and excessive stops.

Finally, because the vehicles are not vans, but buses, the accommodations for conferences and large groups is taken care of. Bill Wheeler has added luxuries on his shuttle service. The buses include televisions, modems, fax machines, and VCRs available en route to the airport. Business time is no longer wasted.

HORSES WORK CLEARING FIREBREAK

Randy Clayton predicted there would be a comeback for working draft horses in the nation's woods and fields. He was right. Clayton and his sturdy animals have returned to the East (San Francisco Bay) hills clearing a firebreak.

Those agencies that manage public lands are now admitting that horses do the same work as machines for about half the price, and with much less damage to the environment. Clayton and his big Belgians appear to be permanently employed.

As if to underscore Clayton's faith in the usefulness of his animals, the East Bay Regional Park District has used goats to clear hilly lands too perilous for humans. The goat owner rents out his four-legged mowers, and collects milk and cheese as well as his rental fees.

ROGUE VALLEY NEWSPAPER FOCUSES ON SPANISH

NUEVA AMANECER, Rogue Valley, one of Oregon's first Spanish language newspapers, is the brainchild of Editor Julietta Espinoza, and her editorial crew,

Virginia Stollings and Beverly Moore. The eight page tabloid bears a mission statement which calls for informing, educating, and entertaining the Spanish-speaking community.

Serving a growing Spanish-speaking population, the publication is attracting corporate support from U.S. West, First Interstate Bank, Valley of the Rogue Bank, and Ike Podaca, president of HISPANA INDUSTRIES, the Rogue Valley's largest Hispanic-owned business.

JUNK YARD EVOLVES INTO
RECYCLING CENTER

Morris Stark, the father, began the business peddling rags, bottles, bones, and scrap metal. From this the venture grew until Morris founded what became EL MONTE IRON AND METAL COMPANY.

When George, the son, picked up the responsibility, he developed the business from its junk yard beginnings to the position of one of the largest recycling centers in Southern California.

El Monte Iron and Metal was recognized in the 1960s by the Johnson Administration as one of the cleanest scrap metal yards in the nation. It was a natural move from a small junk yard to a recycling operation with everything containerized.

RECYCLING BOTTLES PAYS OFF

ENCORE GLASS began as a demonstration project

for the Ecology Center in Berkeley, California. When it became a valid operation, it was split off as a private company.

ENCORE GLASS purchases wine bottles from neighboring community curbside recycling programs, cleaning them and selling them back to wineries. Encore partner, Peter Heylin, reports business is going strong.

Strategy #34

SOLVE GROUP OR PERSONAL NEEDS

Use your good ideas to improve life for others.

ENTREPRENEURS COOK IN RENT-A-KITCHEN

It isn't enough to have a winning recipe for a cookie. You just can't bake a big batch and launch yourself into business. You need a business permit, and a department inspection to determine if your processes are proper, and whether your cookie is safe for human consumption. Your facilities have to pass both county and state health department requirements.

All this becomes frustrating for beginning entrepreneurs hoping to launch their own small businesses. Ann Blakemore, a San Rafael, California, businesswoman knows the trials and tribulations facing a beginner. She knew she had the answer to one of the major problems facing the new food manufacturers – a licensed place to cook.

Thus she opened THE KITCHENS, a busy, five-kitchen cooperative food facility which passes both county and state health department requirements. Ann Blakemore rents the facilities to the new entrepreneurs, and shepherds their efforts. She presently oversees nearly thirty entrepreneurs, all of whom rent time and space in the 4,000 square foot workshop.

GROWING POTENTIAL IN PERSONAL CHEFS

How to squeeze more quality time out of quantity time? The latest trend is to hire the personal chef who shops for the food, cooks approximately two weeks' worth of gourmet meals, packages them up for the freezer, and then cleans up the kitchen afterwards.

"It's a business whose time has come," says David McKay, executive director of the U.S. Personal Chef Association. In market testing, the idea of the Personal Chef proved to be very promising. The association now has chef members in towns of 20,000 to 30,000 and in large cities. Those who want to become personal chefs pay $99 to join, and then buy recipe and training packages at $500 to $1000.

In Spokane, Washington, Sara and Bob Finnigan have set up their service and named it FINNIGAN'S

FEAST. Their infant business in two months grew as fast as they could handle it.

FINNIGAN'S FEAST offers an extensive menu to the customers' personal tastes from a supply of recipes large enough to avoid repeating for six months.

Sara Finnigan reports, "Everyone who's tried it so far has become a long term client." Clients report that having a personal chef has eased stress on a family of working professionals beside saving on restaurant meals and wasted food purchased for home use and never used.

The Finnigans work as a team completing more services by working together. They serve twelve clients now and hope to bump that number up to twenty or twenty-five.

COLEEN'S COOK EASE

In Corvallis, Oregon, Coleen Belisle offers her unique chef services to those who care about what they eat but don't have the time to cook. She goes into a customer's home and cooks a month's supply of entrees. These the customer chooses from Coleen's menu, either regular or low fat, including vegetarian, poultry, and fish dishes.

COLEEN'S COOK EASE complete service covers menu planning, shopping, cooking, packaging, freezing, cleanup, and reheating instructions. At the end of the day,

Coleen offers the client eighty individual servings prepared and packaged for the client's needs.

MADISON AVENUE GIFT BASKETS

Four years ago, Sheri Schweigert struck about for an idea to start a home business. The obvious was baking delicious home made cookies. The place to sell them would be the weekly farmers' market. Her business, called COOKIES FROM HOME, was the natural outcome.

Sheri's cookies were a hit from the start. Drawing on her natural artistic sense of beauty and design, Sheri sold her cookies in miniature decorated shopping bags. This led one customer to suggest she include packets of instant coffee or tea. When Sheri introduced a coffee mug, the bag of cookies was becoming a gift, and a gift seemed to call for a better container.

Among her friends, Sheri had made her reputation for the gifts she gave them. Her gifts were wrapped elegantly in baskets and decorated with flowers, ribbons, and protected with cellophane. What more logical thing than to convert the bag of cookies into baskets of cookies? And to insert special treats or gifts?

Sheri now had her home based business. As her gift baskets were picked up by office workers and professional people, Sheri became less involved in producing cookies and more involved in designing gift baskets featuring gourmet food products. At this juncture, the cookies were baked for Sheri.

Then things got out of hand. Or, rather, the business burst the seams at home. Gift baskets refused to remain confined to a house. Sheri worked herself out of a home based business into a beautiful shop in downtown Corvallis, Oregon.

Today, Sheri has her professionally trained design team to help her create memorable gift baskets by order. The baskets are filled to the customer's taste out of a gourmet selection of foods, wines, bath and baby gifts, candles, cards, books, plants, and cookbooks. Customers, both gift givers and gift receivers, return again and again.

MADISON AVENUE GIFT BASKETS now travel worldwide as local businesses find them excellent gifts to give their own clientele. Sheri somewhat ruefully explains, "It was supposed to be a home-business. I didn't foresee this. It just evolved."

SIGNAGE FOR THE BLIND - A WIDE OPEN MARKET

Ditman Johnson and his wife, Carrie George, bought GARNETT ENGRAVING planning to continue manufacturing the standard brass, aluminum, and vinyl signs that the shop had been producing. Then someone suggested that there might be a market making signs in Braille. There was. An enormous market.

In order to produce raised letter signage, their software, and computer controlled stamping equipment had to be adapted to that kind of production. With this, their new ACCUBRAILLE DIVISION is turning out Braille evacuation maps, roof access signs, elevator buttons, door and restroom signs for hotels, offices, and public buildings.

The demand seems almost unlimited, and the Johnsons are moving into the national market.

TEACHERS FIND TREASURE TROVE IN CHILDREN'S SONGS

Pam Beall and Susan Nipp, former music teachers, felt traditional children's songs were worth saving, so they set out to locate and record the songs that were in the public domain.

From conducting workshops for parents and teachers, they moved into compiling their early collection. Out of that, they self-published 500 copies of a book which they called WEE SING.

Two years later, WEE PUBLISHING, as they named their business, had sold 20,000 copies, and the two teachers began writing and developing a series of nine songbooks for children. Now they continue to develop cassette and video tapes as a standard feature with their song and coloring books.

Although this was not their original reason for collecting children's songs, Susan Nipp and Pam Beall have parlayed their initial $200 investment into a multimillion dollar publishing venture.

```
Strategy #35

CULTIVATE UNIQUE SKILLS
```

If you have a rare skill, you may have little or no competition. Put that rare skill to use.

HE BECAME THE BICYCLE WIZARD OF MORGAN HILL

Mike Sinyard worked his way through college rebuilding bicycles from flea market parts. After graduation and a European bike tour, he decided to import Italian bicycle parts. He opened his business as SPECIALIZED BICYCLE COMPONENTS, but within two years he realized that he could make better designed parts himself.

His business took off with its mass production of mountain bikes. He now has 170 employees at the Morgan Hill, California, location and a total of 250 companywide.

SPECIALISTS REPAIR ONCE IRREPARABLE OUTDOOR GEAR

Bob Upton, owner of RAINY PASS REPAIR in Seattle, along with Sally Shiver, partner, have established a chokehold on the local market for repairing damaged outdoor equipment. Rainy Pass now has 12 employees.

HE CONTOURS CHAIRS TO FIT

Tucked away in the forest in the Sierra Foothills, Robert Erickson has chosen to make his life among the trees he carefully selects for his craftsmanship. His specialty is tailoring fine museum quality chairs to fit the customer.

AND THIS BUSINESS CONTOURS WHEELCHAIRS TO FIT

Doe Cayting, co-owner of WHEELCHAIRS OF BERKELEY, California, as a teenager, found her career goal with the disabled. She began her advocacy in New York when she worked at a summer camp for the disabled. Following this introduction, she moved to California where she became a rehabilitation assistant at the University of California. Her determination deepened as she worked to help disabled students live independently.

Ultimately she met and married an expert wheelchair repairman, who had worked in a rehab hospital. The two combined their skills, hers making life more livable for the disabled, his modifying the needed equipment specifically to fit the disabled owner.

Now WHEELCHAIRS OF BERKELEY keeps only demonstrators in stock, and does not rent equipment. Instead each chair is customized to maximize the individual's body function and structure. Meanwhile, Doe

Cayting continues pressure on wheelchair manufacturers to make similar adjustments, and pushes medical groups for funding.

HIS PAPERS TELL AMERICA'S STORY

When Ernest Chambers became a customs broker his assignment included refunding of excess duties. Because of his strong interest in American history, he inquired where the Customs Service kept historic documents. He learned they were destroyed every seven years. Since then he has made a hobby of collecting old customs papers, some 26,000 of them. He has made important finds, among them being the original construction papers for the Statue of Liberty.

CLERICAL GARMENTS BECOME COLORFUL

In keeping with the times, The Hand-Weavers Guild of America is turning out peacock hued ministerial garb and religious furnishings to replace the traditional somber solid colors.

HE BRINGS READING ALOUD BACK

Bored and looking for something to break the monotony of a long commute, Craig Black slipped the recording of Orwell's book, *"1984"* into a cassette recorder in his car. Suddenly he found that listening to recorded books could change the exhausting hours on the freeway to rich learning time.

With this discovery, he would carve out a place for himself in the audio publishing industry. Under the name BLACKSTONE AUDIO BOOKS, Craig Black now provides complete versions of classic books in fiction, history, economics, politics, and philosophy.

His mailing list of several thousand customers in 68 countries continues to grow. Through small ads in literary and specialty magazines and a newsprint catalog, Black provides customers information about his releases. Sales have been good, and Black confidently expects his steady stream of audio "readers" to increase.

DESIGNERS ARE INSPIRED BY ANTIQUITIES

Because of the growing interest in archaeology, designers are trying to make their new decorative accessories appear to have been unearthed from an authentic dig. Just being antique is not enough.

JERRYSTYLE is a newly expanded Manhattan store that caters to this taste for the old. Jerry Van Deelen, the owner of the store, is in the vanguard of the look.

GARGOYLES ARE IN

In keeping with the trend to bring the old into today, Bob Noto's stock in trade is antique reproduction, plaster re-creations of ornamental wood and stone pieces. Grotesque and ugly are the fad. These pieces are used as supports for shelves, for bookends, adorn mirrors, hold pencils, or just hung there for wall decoration.

His business, GARGOYLES STUDIO, employs a staff of twenty workers and generates sales of about one million dollars annually.

Strategy #34

TRY VARIATIONS ON A THEME

Make an ordinary activity extraordinary. Giving a dog a bath is ordinary. Make it easier. Going to a wedding reception is commonplace. Do it dramatically. Selling real estate is not unusual. Doing it from a wheelchair, and modifying design to accommodate the customer's wheelchair, is.

DIRTY DOG? PET LAUNDROMATS HELP CLEAN UP

Rhonda Taylor, manager of TROY BOYS YOU DO IT PET WASH, at Martinez, California, says the shop offers a less stressful way to wash pets. Customers can use a shoulder high tub complete with hooks for leashing the pet. The animals are walked into the tub, secured tightly, and bathed under warm water, brushed, and blow-dried. Better still, pet owners don't have to mop up afterwards.

THIS HOTEL GOES TO THE DOGS

Francie Terney's downtown hotel, has the usual

amenities of the better hotels; rooms painted in soft pastels, comfortable beds, healthy food, and a window with a view. In addition, there is the sound of TV in each room, and facilities for exercise.

Francie is a fussy hostess. No guest can check in without a thorough scrubbing and a shampoo. Dirty dogs need not apply.

Francie, you see, owns and operates TERNEY'S DOG GROOMING AND HOTEL in downtown Pendleton, Oregon. Francie began grooming dogs in her home 12 years ago.

Keeping dogs clean and comfortable is her intention, and to this end, she opened her Dog Hotel, with nine rooms set aside for the pampered pets, as a replacement for the less elegant kennels. Francie enforces the cleanliness and grooming regularly with two to four dogs a day combed, clipped, bathed, and blow dried.

The business is doing well in spite of the community controversy swirling around city hall over the hotel's location and definition.

STOPPING THE NICKEL-AND-DIME LOSSES

Good managers are always concerned with waste in their businesses, but seldom do they look at the tiny leaks. Bob Lonkart and John Marshall under the name of COST MANAGEMENT ASSOCIATES, Providence, Rhode Island, have made it their goal to go into the small purchases and expenditure services that cut into the profit margins.

Office supplies, light bulbs, local and long distance phone calls, express mail charges, and paper costs, are some of the items that are responsible for an excessive leakage. For thirteen customers alone, Lonkart and Marshall saved a minimum of $300,000. That's for the year they were hired. Afterwards clients can continue to save by following their advice.

HE THRIVES ON CHALLENGES

Neal Smither is a real estate broker in El Sobrante, California, which, on the surface is not particularly noteworthy until you learn the challenges he faced.

He has a life of accomplishment in spite of being paralyzed in an accident. The co-owner of PRIME PROPERTIES REALTY COMPANY and owner of PREMIUM MORTGAGE COMPANY, in addition to being a developer and builder, Smither has achieved remarkable financial independence through the use of his solid innovative skills.

His unique specialty is accommodating houses to the needs of owners who are also wheelchair bound.

SUMMARY

Willingness to learn is essential to success in creating a small business. If you prefer to bypass all the learning necessary to start and conduct a business of your own, the safest investment is to set up a lemonade stand in the front yard. Then, when sales drop off, you can drink up your inventory and move on to other activities.

On the other hand, people who make their ideas their business and persist in the pursuit of their goals are the hope of the future.

As long as the inflow of new ideas overbalances discouragement and depression, this right balance of thinking will bring out progress. Count on it.

PLAN NO. 12

YOU'RE ON YOUR OWN

You've decided to start a small business. Good. You've decided what that business will be. Good. At this point, you have taken the first (just the first) steps toward your own business. Now the watchword is: proceed cautiously.

If you still hold a job, keep on holding it. Start your small business as a fall back plan. Your job will make it possible to build a new business without risking your savings. This is very important during a time of economic uncertainty. When your infant business can stand alone, then is the time to quit your job.

Learn as much as you can about your kind of business before you open the doors. It's easier and less expensive to correct mistakes before you make a serious investment. Find out the pros and cons of what you propose to do.

Take advantage of the community colleges and the adult courses they offer, courses in planning a small business, in advertising and marketing, in accounting, in management, and business law.

Take a class in developing business plans. Learn about costs and how to control them. Learn what start up expenses might be and the day-to-day maintenance costs. Find out how to budget for them. Learn how to price your service or product.

There are a number of excellent resources for helpful facts and figures. Many are governmental agencies and their assistance is usually free or inexpensive. You will want to know zoning ordinances and licensing requirements. Go to city agencies for information that will help you. Use the state agencies for the same purpose.

Check with the Better Business Bureau for their services.

Check with the Chamber of Commerce for information about any information and assistance they can offer. Learn about Enterprise Zones and Business Enterprise Centers. Find out what your bank has to offer. Banks often distribute pamphlets that are helpful to the businesses in the area. Take advantage of these.

It would be worth your time to make a trip to the nearest office of the Small Business Administration. At the least, call or write them for information. Here you will find free and for sale booklets on starting and running a small business. Get whatever applies to you. Ask about the loan plans available. Ask, too, about SCORE, a counseling service offered by retired executives for the small business owner.

Once you open your business, remember you are learning a new skill, the skill of creating a small business. Be patient with the business and with yourself. Be persistent while you are learning. It takes time to develop and establish a business. Don't let discouragement defeat you just as you are beginning to succeed.

Strategy No. 37

PLAN FOR SUCCESS

Be businesslike from the start. Maintain definite hours. Answer inquiries promptly. Keep accurate records. These are essential for financial reports to give you a reading on the strengths and weaknesses of your business. Of course, complete records are vital for taxation purposes.

Give the best product or best service you can. Build your business reputation on quality. That, plus friendliness, will attract customers.

You are now the owner-manager, the boss. You wanted to be the decision maker. Well, now you are. Some decisions you make will be good. Some will create problems for you. The mistakes you make will force your growth. That, in itself, is good.

You have joined a great army of movers and shakers. These are the entrepreneurs without which our nation would not prosper. Your small business will help build a safer future.

Hang in there. We need you. Courage in hand, you walk the road to success.

PLAN NO. 13

WATCH FOR SIGNS OF THE TIMES

Ask any gardener. His crops are abundant when the climate is right. The same goes for jobs. Watch for those signs which indicate the growth of new jobs. This changing world is creating new demands.

Strategy No. 38

TURN PROBLEMS INTO OPPORTUNITIES

Here are some of them:

AGRICULTURE

*   The biotechnology of genetic engineering promises to expand agriculture from supplying food and fibers to a greatly enlarged potential of new materials. Among these are the plants that have pharmaceutical applications.

*   Biotechnology offers the possibility for crops leading to cheap, biodegradable plastics, and also bio-fuels.

*   The biotech industry in all its phases has trouble meeting its manpower needs.

*   Jobs as gardeners and groundskeepers are abundant.

*   There is a growing tendency for farmers to branch out into additional activities that are more lucrative. Some are opening small food stands, pancake houses, setting up agricultural welding as a sideline, making quilts or other crafts for sale, even providing computer services to neighbors. One has set up a family farm with a restaurant. He lectures on farm diversification at conferences, and acts as a representative for a factory which manufactures plastic jugs for maple syrup.

*   The concept of farmer's markets is growing rapidly from its early beginnings at the roadside stand. Now family owned farms are finding eager customers for their produce in urban areas, especially when the weekly market is located in malls or near rapid transit stations.

*   A number of the vendors specialize in organic produce, that is, their produce is raised without chemicals. From a scant number of idealistic farmers, organic gardening is now expanding into a multimillion dollar industry.

Other vendors bring in dried fruits, honey, nuts, bakery items, specialty vegetables, and herbs. In some farmers' markets, craft vendors are welcome to set up displays.

So enthusiastic are both sellers and buyers, that some farmers' markets find they need to retain the services of a farmers' markets consultant. The consultant works to maintain a balance of vendors. The aim is to complement but not compete with nearby regular merchants.

COMPUTER

* The potential for computer software is limitless

* Computer simulators offer a new learning tool for training employees.

* Beyond the computer games is the potential for expanding into better educational software.

* Computer systems analysts are first on a list of fastest growing professions, followed by electronic equipment repair people.

* Computer programmers rank high on the demand list.

* Computer repair people and people in research and development will continue to find work.

COMMUNICATIONS

* The growth of computers has led to the concept of the Information Super Highway, a metaphor to describe the idea of linking homes and businesses everywhere. In a newsletter to its members, the PIONEER TELEPHONE COOPERATIVE, Philomath, Oregon, says of the Information Super Highway, "This leads to unlimited possibilities." Some of them are:

* "A global computer network linking educational facilities, government, businesses, and even the individual homeowner, giving users access to library databases, electronic bulletin boards, electronic mail, and other sources of information.

* "Video on demand. Video phones/video conferencing.

* "Telemedicine

* "Interactive Television

* "Telecommuting

* "Home shopping

* "The communications revolution will spawn broad changes in telephone companies, cable television companies, wireless companies, broadcasters, and electric utilities."

EDUCATION AND TRAINING

*   High schools are reorganizing into smaller mini-schools that focus on career paths.

*   New methods for securing the safety of students from violence in the schools will be developed. One unique aspect has been the Security Dads program which brings male parents into the activities. This may evolve into paid positions.

*   Instead of just learning theory, new classes emphasize hands on training in chemistry and physics, using materials they will deal with on the job.

*   The training of manufacturing workers will start with apprentice programs for students of high school age to ease the school to work transition. Flexible factories need adaptable workers who can work in teams, and have the self-sufficiency to acquire new skills as needed.

*   New jobs are appearing at the Document Design Center in Washington, D.C. in which English majors work at translating government gobbledygook into plain English. This trend should eventually expand into translating technical manuals into English that nontechnical people can understand.

*   Adult learners expect that classes will provide them with practical information they need. Instructors must not only be educators, but have the practical experience that makes their teaching vital.

*   The increased tendency toward home schooling will require development of teaching materials for use at home.

*   Television classes will become more available as adults demand more accessibility to learning.

*   Latin is returning to the classroom. There is a scarcity of Latin teachers. Foreign languages of all kinds are becoming a necessity in international trade. Instructors are needed.

*   The United States is behind in engineering, computer science, electronics, communications, robotics, and instrumentation. Specialists in these fields will be needed as instructors.

*   College will go to the workplace via "brown-bag seminars."

*   Educational courses for RNs and many other health-care jobs, courses such as nursing, respiratory therapy, medical terminology, medical insurance and billing, are doing a booming business.

*   Colleges are adding gerontology as well as alcohol and drug studies.

ENABLING THE DISABLED

*   The Americans with Disabilities Act is fueling the effort to produce publications for the blind and visually impaired.

* Jobs will develop with construction companies to make the building modifications which allow access to all public accommodations for people with disabilities.

* Inventions are needed which make it possible for the disabled to be more mobile, thus increasing their chances for employment.

* Inventors in the field of ergonomics for the disabled are greatly needed. Ergonomics is the science of designing products to work with people, matching aspects of the individual, like arm length, for instance, to product design.

ENERGY

* Wind energy is becoming a viable resource for utilities. Jobs will appear in the manufacture of the energy producing turbines and their installation.

* Any new energy source will generate power and jobs.

* Fuel cell technology, clean, quiet, flexible, is about to leave obscurity for mainstream use.

ENGINEERS

* Environmental engineers are needed to clean up waste product repositories.

* Structural design and stress analysis engineers are in short supply.

*   Electronics equipment repairmen are in demand.

ENVIRONMENT

*   Environmentalists are beginning to create an ecological data base to allow access to a region's changing biodiversity.

*   Sealed buildings create a new industry industrial hygiene.

*   More jobs will open up in the removal of underground storage tanks, and soil remediation.

*   Jobs in the development and installation of wastewater treatment systems are expected to increase.

*   There is a growing demand for waste water testing and therefore for scientists with this specialty.

*   Rail business is growing because of the new trend to move trash and garbage by train to new landfills.

*   Pilot tree planting programs to test low cost methods of reducing carbon dioxide will need tree planters. Restoration of our forests will open more tree planting jobs.

*   Environmental jobs are evolving: setting up plastics recycling program, establishing nature conservancies, building electric cars, environmental management in solid waste.

*   Jobs are opening up in developing alternatives to wood.

*   The EPA has toughened its standards on vehicle emissions. This means more jobs in vehicle testing programs. It is estimated repair work generated by the tests will require between 3,800 and 11,600 additional workers.

*   Polluters, whether individuals, corporations, or governmental agencies, will be required to clean up environmental damage from chemicals. Jobs in cleanup will increase.

EXPANDED MINORITY BUSINESS

*   As minority businesses increase, they will hire more. The ability to speak a second language will be important.

*   Minority publishers say revenues are up. There is a growing demand for publications serving minority populations.

*   Women, especially minority women, are opening many small businesses. If the business prospers, jobs will open up.

HEALTH AND MEDICAL FIELDS

*   A growing national interest in fitness is creating jobs for college graduates in commercial and industrial fitness. Corporations, fitness clubs, clinical settings,

and others are interested in physical fitness for themselves or their employees. Business and industry recruiters are looking for potential managers in the area of exercise and sport science.

* The health care sector has ongoing shortages for positions such as physical therapists, physical therapist assistants, physical therapy aides, medical records technicians, paramedics, respiratory therapists, an X-ray technicians.

* Jobs abound for registered nurses and pharmacists.

* Health care jobs are found in emergency room, critical care, community health, and pediatrics settings.

* Instead of buying traditional health insurance for their employees, businesses have begun to enroll in managed health care programs. Health maintenance organizations provide medical care to the employees .

* Nurses are working in a range of profitable health care related businesses. They are writing software programs for medical enterprises. Nurses are running cardiovascular monitoring and rehabilitation centers, and designing health care facilities. They are also serving as legal consultants on complex malpractice or personal injury lawsuits.

* Fast-growing occupations include home health care aides, medical assistant radiologic technicians, and medical secretaries.

HOUSING

* The shortage of affordable housing points to a need for better financing and an explosive rate of construction in the near future.

* There is a trend toward 'live-in/work-in' space.This new term means remodeling buildings in industrial areas to provide living quarters upstairs and work areas below. Living in the workplace is not a new idea, of course. 'Live-in/work-in' has the potential to eliminate the stressful elements of commuter life. Jobs in remodeling are increasing.

INFRASTRUCTURE

* Large public investment is inevitable as bridges and highways continue to deterio-rate at a rapid rate. The reconstruction will generate thousands of jobs in roads, rail, airports, water systems, sewage treatment, and power facilities.

* Workers will be assigned to civilian projects. These include a national high speed rail system, highway and bridge repair, job retraining, and research to develop new products.

* There will be heavy demand to clean up and restore large communities hit by fire, earthquake, hurricanes, and floods.

INTERNATIONAL TRADE

*   As international trade becomes more prevalent, specialists will be needed to conduct seminars on business cultures of other nations.

JOB RETRAINING

*   There is a great need for practical solutions to the retraining of all displaced workers. The Job Training Partnership Act (JTPA) money helps to fund programs that provide job counseling, retraining, and placement assistance. Program developers and instructors are needed.

*   PACIFIC GAS AND ELECTRIC COMPANY (California) has opened a construction training center which not only teaches basic electrical theory, but also trains new workers on actual job skills.

*   Company operated training schools will become increasingly necessary.

KIN-CARE CAREGIVERS

*   The expansion of health care services provided outside hospitals has increased the need for occupational and physical therapists, and critical care nurses.

*   Child care has a chronic shortage of trained workers.

*   Upscale restaurants are considering providing baby sitting to relieve parents of the chaos which usually ensues when eating out with children.

*   Eldercare will include adult foster home Care workers are in demand. Adult day care represents a huge business opportunity.

*   A new kind of entrepreneur is evolving: the 'doula'. The doula provides in-home postpartum care to help the new mother through the period immediately after childbirth.

*   Organizing seniors' affairs is turning into a growth industry. Small businesses handling the financial affairs of seniors are sprouting up around the country.

LANGUAGES

*   Bilingual businessmen believe Spanish will be the most important foreign language for a successful business career. Jobs are available for those fluent in Spanish.

*   U.S. has the fifth largest number of Spanish speakers in the world after Mexico, Spain, Argentina, and Colombia. This will be intensified by the new trade agreement with Mexico. Teaching jobs will develop for those educators whose specialty is Spanish.

*   American Telephone and Telegraph Company's Language Line provides interpreters who speak most common languages. If you have a second language, (Language Line uses more than 140 languages), you may find your job based on your language talents.

*   "The globalization of our economy and greater

interdependence between countries will make knowledge of a second language a key asset in the next decade", said Max Messmer, chairman of ACCOUNTEMPS. Foreign language skills are in demand.

* Esperanto, invented in 1887 as a universal second language and a bridge between all the world's cultures, is now experiencing a revival as a language that builds bridges between nations. Miko Sloper, office director of the Esperanto League for North America, says, "Esperanto is a truly neutral language that is owned by no nation."

LAW ENFORCEMENT

* Spanish speaking police officers are needed to deal with problems arising from the growing Spanish speaking public.

* There is a great need for more trained safety inspectors to monitor refineries, chemical plants, and other dangerous industrial operations.

* With the stability of our financial institutions in question, there is a need for bank examiners, according to the FDIC.

OPPORTUNITIES IN GENERAL

* Demand occupations: paralegals (legal assistants), truck drivers, cosmetologists, diesel mechanics, heating and air conditioning mechanics, upholsterers.

PRIVATIZATION

*   "Shortfalls in government revenues are likely to lead to a greater level of 'privatization' of such publicly owned and operated facilities as prisons, schools, water and waste utilities," says the FIRST INTERSTATE BANCORP FORECAST.

*   With the enormous national debt and lower revenues, the government is trying to cut costs by turning to private industry to provide basic services. Services that once were exclusively the province of the government are now being handled by private agencies. Contact them for potential jobs.

RECYCLING

*   Recycling has become good business. When a developer recycles right at the site, he saves money in dump fees and transportation costs. One developer reports on-site recycling of concrete, asphalt, and wood. Moving and replanting large trees saved the considerable cost of new trees. There will be a growing trend toward on site recycling and the jobs necessary to do it.

*   The pulp and paper business has entered the recycling business in a bigger way as demand for the recycled materials increases. Jobs evolve from what used to be dumped in the landfills.

*   The Environmental Protection Agency wants public advice on how to encourage recycling of used oil, and comments on rules for storage and disposal of used oil.

*   Recycling business development activities along an industrial shoreline will create more jobs and less garbage for the area.

*   Field tests are being conducted to break down used tires into "crumb rubber" to be used in asphalt paving. Rubber chips are used for manufacturing products like pickup truck bed liners and impact mouldings. New jobs in manufacturing are possible.

*   Plastic lumber plants will benefit plastic recycling programs throughout the country. Plastic lumber can be used in marinas, public parks, and in parking lots. It is hoped a new sorting machinery now being developed will encourage recycling efforts.

TRANSPORTATION

*   A great many changes are ahead in the transportation industry. There will be creation of several new technologies.

*   High-speed transportation systems will include bullet trains.

*   Super speed electric trains are expected to link cities.

*   There will be development of motor vehicles using alternative fuels. Among these are more sophisticated electric cars.

TRAVEL

* The travel industry is enjoying a robust economy. Work as a travel professional is taking of. Senior travel companies expand tours and cruises adapted to the growing market of active seniors, with a range of travel styles and preferences.

* A strong market for ecotourism has developed. Suzanne K. Eggleston, editor of the magazine ECO TRAVELER says the market is measurable in the millions. This for of travel is devoted to exploring natural wonders, and exotic cultures.

WATER AND WASTE WATER TREATMENT

* Mobile water treatment plants are the wave of the future.

* New waste water treatment systems will clean water better and more rapidly. There is a growing potential for more jobs in this field.

The foregoing trends are only a portion of the amazing transformations taking place right now in this country's businesses and industries. Although there may be a great deal of disruption at present, thousands of new occupations are evolving in answer to the challenge.

SUMMARY

Ultimately, when we change our focus from pleasure seeking to problem solving, every one will have a job.

PLAN NO. 14

MANAGE YOUR OWN JOB SEARCH

Now, a few words to shore up your confidence: Do you want a job? You have one. To be employed means to be busy. Managing your own job search will keep you busy. If properly done, it should also bring you a comfortable income.

You are an individual with the power to think and act for yourself. The minute you apply these thoughts and energies to managing your own life, you are no longer unemployed. True, for the present you may be unpaid, but not unemployed...not without work.

Stop thinking of yourself as cast adrift. Forget luck, either good or bad. Nobody ever succeeded by believing he was at the mercy of mysterious forces. Get off your knees. You are not dependent on the whims of others.

Know what you want. Know what you can do. Know what the employer wants. Then figure out the best way to use this knowledge to your benefit.

The employer is not a fire-breathing dragon. He is not a benevolent dictator, nor a walking welfare agency.

An employer gets headaches, argues with his (or her) spouse, and bleeds when wounded.

Scratch an employer and you will find a human being. Because he is human, he is apt to have biases, and sometimes he is downright unreasonable. He (or she) is also vulnerable. He has his own goals and suffers his own defeats. On occasion he succeeds. He also fails.

To increase the successes and reduce the possibility of failures, the employers hope to hire employees with confidence and reliability. Obviously, then, you should exude confidence and reliability. Accept the fact that you have the power to think correctly and then act upon these thoughts.

No single employer nor one occupation is the sole solution to your need for a job. Placing all your expectations in one event is tunnel vision. Only one possibility for you? Nonsense. Your horizons are almost unlimited if you do your required homework.

On the job you expected to put in forty or more hours a week. You may not have that job any more. Instead, you are in business for yourself...the business of selling your talents...on a commission basis. The payoff will be the job. Are you going to short change yourself? You need your good work habits more than ever now.

If you were being hired to look for a job, the employer would expect you to work at that job forty hours a week. Hire yourself, and do the job expected of you–forty hours a week.

It is not enough to uncover ten, twenty, or thirty hidden jobs. Planting an application does not insure sprouting a job. You cannot afford the luxury of inactivity. For the time being you may have to adjust your life style to the inconvenience of being unpaid, but sitting around, waiting for others to rescue you from stagnation, is the sure road to failure.

Keep in mind; It is far preferable to do something imperfectly than to do nothing at all.

Strategy No. 39

ESTABLISH A CONFIDENT OUTLOOK

Take control. Sit down and plan first. Hold off applying for jobs until you know where you are headed and why.

You are now in the business of selling a product...your talents. Know your product thoroughly. This means you must identify your skills. Be certain of their value. If you don't think they are any good, why on earth would you expect an employer to pay money for them?

Know how these assets (your skills) can be used to the employer's advantage. Know several names (job titles) for this aggregation of tasks.

You spend a large part of your life at work. The proper work for you must be that in which you can use your skills, strength, and intelligence. If you don't know what this work is, get to a career counselor immediately. Usually you will find help at a college class or career center. Try the library for books in career choice. Know what you want. Don't expect an employment interviewer to do this for you. He is neither a career counselor, nor does he have a crystal ball.

Now that you have identified the kind (or kinds) of work you do well, line up facts to prove to yourself and, ultimately, to an employer that you can do the job.

If you are doubtful or uncertain about your abilities, your doubt and uncertainty will show, and the employer will not be convinced. When you apply for a position, you are offering your services. If you have only superficial reasons why you will be a good candidate, you sell yourself short, and the employer won't buy.

Next, consider your surroundings. Ask yourself: "What kind of company, big or small, do I want to work for? What company and management philosophy will promote my development? What kind of associates are appropriate for me?"

Investigate the company thoroughly. The company will certainly investigate you. Look for length of time in business, rate of growth, research and development programs, future potential, and financial rating. Analyze the advertising program. It reveals company attitudes.

And speaking of advertising...how do you advertise yourself? Is your résumé up-to-date? If you have one that is the old chronological style, the answer is, "No", even if you have included recent experience.

Do you know how to compose an effective résumé? If not, then attend business or adult classes to learn how, or consult a specialist in resume writing...**writing** (composing), not **typing**.

Do you have trouble presenting your ideas in interviews? Correct this deficiency immediately. Again, take classes to learn how. If no classes are available, get some current books at the library on effective interviewing techniques.

While you are there, check out a book or two written for the benefit of the employer. Here you will find questions you may later be asked, and with them the expected correct reply. You will learn, too, about interview rating systems, so these will not come as an unwelcome surprise.

Take the time to write down a list of questions you would ask if you had to interview an applicant for the job you are seeking. Now, can you answer these questions clearly and precisely? Practice talking out the answers in front of a mirror. Watch out for annoying mannerisms. Remember to smile. You are not facing a firing squad.

Are you working eight hours a day on these various projects? You should be. When you are not listing your talents, you should be listing employers and learning contact names. When you are not attending classes to polish your presentation, you should be mapping out your search territory. When you are not composing résumés (yes, more than one…no résumé is an all-purpose garment), you should draw up cover letters to go with the résumés.

Meanwhile there are thirty-nine hidden job strategies to follow and you need to do in-depth research of every employer for which you want to work.

By now, you can see, you already have full-time employment. When you feel reasonably confident that you can tell an employer 1) why you want that job, 2) why you know you can handle it, 3) why you want to work for him, 4) why you believe you will be a benefit to the company, then you are ready to apply for the job.

Whether your first stop is the state employment service, a private agency, or the employer's front door, go properly groomed. First impressions on placement or employment interviewers are as vital as those on the employer. These impressions can make or break you. The employment interviewer must make referrals that please the employer. If you arrive at his desk dressed sloppily or inappropriately, he will look for a better qualified applicant.

Explain clearly to the interviewer at the employment service office or private agency what it is you are looking for as your job goal. Marshal all your facts before you fill out your application. Take a résumé or a neatly typed fact sheet to help the interviewer.

Go often enough so the interviewer gets to know you by name and sight. He is then likely to recall you when a suitable job opening comes up. Establish a friendly relationship with the interviewer. Keep this relationship alive.

It is all right to be willing to take intermediate steps such as an interim job which shows promise of leading to your ultimate goal, but don't let the interviewer talk you into applying for a position about which you feel uneasy. If you do, you may end up shortly redoing the whole employment process.

Once you have been interviewed by an employer for his job opening, follow up. Write a thank-you note after the interview. Include additional pertinent information if appropriate. Continue to follow up in person or by phone. A good position is worth expending effort to get.

Those applicants who are offered jobs are not necessarily the most qualified. A pleasant personality and prompt follow-up has landed many a good job for less qualified, but persistent applicants.

Diplomatic persistence, enthusiasm, and drive will pay off. Keep going back until you get a definite answer. If you are hired, you can then channel your efforts toward the work you will be doing. If the answer is "No", then you are free to apply your efforts looking elsewhere.

Time spent in searching for work is extremely valuable and should not be wasted. And finally...

* Learn to depend upon yourself.

* Trust your talents.

* Learn to smile.

* Get along with others.

* Don't be afraid to be different.

* Look ahead.

* Persist.

* When you control your own destiny...

**YOU HAVE AN APPOINTMENT
WITH SUCCESS.**

About the author

Violet M. Cooper is a professional career counselor, lecturer, employment counselor, and newspaper columnist. She founded her own business, **Career Management Associates,** to specialize in developing unique methods for career choice and job-getting. *HOW TO FIND THOSE HIDDEN JOBS* is the result.

INDEX

216

220

222

224

225